THE·
SCARLET
LETTER

A Reading

TWAYNE'S MASTERWORK STUDIES

Robert Lecker, General Editor

The Bible: A Literary Study
John H. Gottcent

Moby-Dick: Ishmael's Mighty Book
Kerry McSweeney

THE
SCARLET
LETTER

A Reading

NINA BAYM

TWAYNE PUBLISHERS • BOSTON
A Division of G. K. Hall & Co.

The Scarlet Letter: A Reading
Nina Baym

Twayne's Masterwork Studies
No. 1

Copyright © 1986 by G. K. Hall & Co.
All Rights Reserved
Published by Twayne Publishers
A Division of G. K. Hall & Co.
70 Lincoln Street, Boston, Massachusetts 02111

All quotations from The Scarlet Letter are taken from the Centenary
Edition, vol. 1, published by the Ohio State University Press, 1962. Letters
quoted in "The Critical Reception" are taken from volume 16 of the
Centenary Edition, Letters 1843–1853 (1985), 311–12 and 421.

Copyediting supervised by Lewis DeSimone
Designed and produced by Marne B. Sultz
Typeset in 10/14 Sabon with Cloister
Display type by Compset, Inc.

Printed on permanent/durable acid-free paper
and bound in the United States of America

First Paperback Edition

Library of Congress Cataloging-in-Publication Data

Baym, Nina.
The scarlet letter.

(Twayne's masterwork studies ; no. 1)
Bibliography: p. 109
Includes index.
1. Hawthorne, Nathaniel, 1804–1864. Scarlet letter.
I. Title.   II. Series.
PS1868.B39   1986   813'.3   86-9774
ISBN 0-8057-7959-4
ISBN 0-8057-8001-7 (pbk)

Contents

A READING

1.
WHAT? THE STORY   1
On the threshold · A story begins
The plot thickens · Plot and structure

2.
WHERE? THE SETTING   30
The historical setting · The marvelous
and the symbolic · The narrator

3.
WHO? THE CHARACTERS   52
The Puritans · Pearl · Chillingworth
Hester · Dimmesdale · Hawthorne
as psychologist

Chronology of Nathaniel Hawthorne's Life

1801 2 August:	In the seaport town of Salem, Massachusetts, Nathaniel Hathorne, Sr., from a seafaring family and a sea captain himself, marries Elizabeth Clarke Manning, one of nine children of Miriam Lord and Richard Manning, an up-and-coming merchant. The couple moves in with Hathorne's widowed mother and his two sisters. (Nathaniel Hawthorne, Jr., added the *w* to his family name when he began to publish.)
1802 7 March:	Elizabeth Manning Hathorne, their first child, born while Nathaniel Hathorne is away at sea.
1804 4 July:	Nathaniel born. His father is again away and does not return until October, remaining in Salem only briefly.
1808 9 January:	A third child, Maria Louisa, born. Nathaniel Hathorne is at sea. March: Hathorne, Sr., dies of yellow fever, in Surinam; in seven years of married life, he has been at home for about seven months total. July: Elizabeth Hathorne returns to live with her natal family, the Mannings, among whom her three children are to grow up.
1813	Grandfather Manning dies, and Uncle Richard Manning moves to Raymond, Maine, to manage family property there.
1813–1815	A foot injury is slow to mend, keeping Nathaniel from active play and friendships for about two years. During this time he develops a love for reading, especially story books.
1818	Elizabeth and the children move to Raymond also. Nathaniel returns to Salem during winters for schooling, but misses the wilderness and freedom of Maine.

1821	Enters Bowdoin College in Brunswick, Maine. Much to his distress, his mother and sisters return to Salem.
1825	Graduates from college and returns to Salem. He has decided to become a writer.
1825–1837	Lives at home in Salem (his grandmother, as well as several aunts and uncles, have died or moved out) and works at his writing. He changes the spelling of his last name and reads widely in contemporary periodicals and New England history, which he uses as the basis for some of his most successful stories. Somewhat reclusive during this period, he sends his sister Elizabeth to the Salem Athenaeum to withdraw the books and magazines he wants to read.
1828	Anonymous publication of *Fanshawe: A Tale*, a short novel. In later life he never mentions this work; only his sister Elizabeth knows or remembers that he wrote it.
1830–1837	Begins to publish tales and sketches, anonymously, in periodicals.
1836	Edits, with sister Elizabeth's help, the *American Magazine of Useful and Entertaining Knowledge*, in an attempt to establish a literary career.
1837	Writes, with sister Elizabeth's help, *Peter Parley's Universal History*, another attempt to support himself as a literary man.
1837	Brings out *Twice-Told Tales*, a selection from his previously published sketches and tales, under his own name. The book does not sell well but it is widely and favorably reviewed. Elizabeth Palmer Peabody, a gregarious social reformer and fellow Salemite, seeks him out and begins to introduce him to people in her circle, including her younger sister Sophia.
1838	Nathaniel and Sophia become secretly engaged. Begins to publish in a new political journal, the *United States Magazine and Democratic Review*; most of his work published between 1838 and 1845 appears in this magazine.
1839–1840	Financial security through literary projects having thus far failed him, Hawthorne accepts a political appoint-

ment, obtained through friends in the Democratic party, as measurer of salt and coal at the Boston customhouse.

1841   Publishes *Grandfather's Chair*, a history, for children, of New England from the Puritan settlement through the Revolution, which he had written while working at the Boston customhouse. From April to November lives at the experimental Brook Farm community at West Roxbury, Massachusetts, still hoping to find a way to support himself without giving up his literary goals; discovers that he is too exhausted and distracted to write there.

1842 9 July: Marries Sophia Peabody. Moves to Concord, Massachusetts, where he lives at the Old Manse and comes to know major figures in the American Transcendental movement—Ralph Waldo Emerson, Henry David Thoreau, and Margaret Fuller, among others. A second and expanded edition of *Twice-Told Tales* is issued, as well as *Biographical Stories for Children*. He writes regularly for periodicals, but is still unable to make a living as a writer.

1844 March: A daughter, Una, born. Later in the year poverty forces the family to break up briefly: Sophia goes to her parents, who have moved to Boston; Nathaniel returns to his mother and sisters in Salem.

1846 June: A son, Julian, born; a new book of collected sketches and tales, *Mosses from an Old Manse*, published. In the autumn the family settles in Salem, where Hawthorne accepts a political appointment as surveyor in the customhouse.

1849 June: A new political administration dismisses Hawthorne from the customhouse. July: death of Hawthorne's mother. September: begins to write *The Scarlet Letter*.

1850   Moves to Lenox, Massachusetts; meets and becomes friends with Herman Melville and has considerable influence on the writing of *Moby-Dick*, which comes out at the end of the year. March: *The Scarlet Letter* is published by the Boston firm of Ticknor, Reed, and Fields, who will remain Hawthorne's American publishers for the rest of his life.

1851   Moves to West Newton, Massachusetts. May: Rose, third and last child, born. Publishes *The House of the Seven Gables* (a novel), *The Snow-Image and Other Twice-Told Tales* (a collection of stories and sketches), and *True Stories from History and Biography* (a second set of biographies, for children, of famous people).

1852   Moves to the Wayside, in Concord, Massachusetts. Publishes *The Blithedale Romance* (a novel), *A Wonder-Book for Girls and Boys* (retellings of classical myths for children), and a campaign biography of his college friend Franklin Pierce, who is elected president of the United States. July: his sister Maria Louisa is drowned in a steamboat explosion.

1853   Publishes *Tanglewood Tales for Girls and Boys*, a second book of classical myths retold for children. Appointed consul at Liverpool, England, by President Franklin Pierce. Has hopes at last of being financially secure.

1853–1857   Lives in England during consular service. Keeps extensive notebooks but finds it impossible to do any sustained and publishable writing.

1857–1859   Pierce is not reelected, and Hawthorne's term as consul ends. He lives in Rome and Florence, beginning *The Marble Faun*, which will be his last novel, in 1858. Toward the end of this period Una becomes seriously ill with malaria and almost dies. The family is permanently affected by this near tragedy.

1859   After Una's recovery, the family returns to England, where Hawthorne completes and publishes *The Marble Faun*.

1860   Returns to the United States and the Wayside, which he buys and remodels. *The Marble Faun* is published in the United States.

1860–1864   Tries unsuccessfully to write another long work of fiction, producing drafts and fragments of three different romances. He also prepares and publishes essays on England drawn from notebook materials. His health begins to fail.

1863   *Our Old Home*, collecting his English essays, is published. He dedicates the book to Franklin Pierce, an un-

	wise although loyal personal gesture in the midst of the Civil War, when the Democratic party is much out of favor in the North.
1864 19 May:	Dies away from home while on a brief vacation with Franklin Pierce. Buried on 23 May.

Nathaniel Hawthorne
1804–1864
Portrait by Charles Osgood, 1840
Courtesy of the Essex Institute, Salem, Mass.

The Historical Context

Viewed from one perspective, the nation during the years of Hawthorne's adulthood—say, from 1825 to his death—enjoyed ideological consensus and cultural harmony; viewed from another, it was mired in turbulence and conflict. On the one hand, Americans were mostly of the same English or Scottish ethnic background; they lived between the Mississippi River and the Atlantic Ocean on farms or in small towns (in 1840 only Baltimore, Philadelphia, New York, and Boston had populations above 100,000) sharing agrarian, free-enterprise, and egalitarian values; they were passionately nationalistic—protectionist with respect to Europe, expansionist with respect to the American continent. If few people were rich, few lived in deep poverty; most hoped for simple comfort and material security rather than great luxury. They tempered their individualism with strong community values; they were optimistic believers in hard work, education, and the inevitable connection between virtue, moderation, and success.

On the other hand, Americans were divided between slave and free states, were engaged in massive relocation and extermination of the continent's Native American population, and were torn between an economy based on ownership of land and one based on control of money. In the 1840s reform movements proliferated, and utopian community experiments sprang up across the nation, signs of social malaise. Schisms within the established religious denominations, and new sects also appeared in great numbers; evangelical and highly emotional religious behavior began to replace the more sedate practices of the established churches. The political party structure, reflecting constant realignment of interests, changed in fifty years from the opposition of Federalists versus Democratic Republicans, to Whigs versus Democrats, to Democrats versus Republicans (along with various shorter-lived third parties); the Democratic party evolved from the "progressive" party of business and money to the "conservative" party of landowners and slaveholders.

During Hawthorne's lifetime there were three wars (the War of 1812, the Mexican War, and the Civil War), constant skirmishes in the border states between defenders and opponents of slavery, and continual violence between settlers and Indians on the frontier. Severe economic depressions in 1815, 1837, and 1857 threw thousands out of work and sent numerous displaced farm families into rapidly expanding urban slums, there to mingle uncomfortably with newly arriving immigrants from Ireland, Germany, and Scandinavia. New Englanders especially left the poor soil and smallholdings of their native region for new lives on the celebrated frontier, all too often only to meet conditions of disease and extreme physical hardship for which they were completely unprepared. New England, with its religious and moralistic approach to life's problems, lost out to the much more secular and cosmopolitan New York City as the center of the nation's intellectual life, while the South retreated ever more into its own separatist culture. Already, by 1850—less than sixty years after the establishment of the Constitution—one could hear, side by side with expressions of the most intense national boosterism, the lament that Americans had lost their sense of national purpose and had rejected the original values that had made the country so promising.

In the early years of the nineteenth century, when Hawthorne was a boy, the profession of authorship underwent a dramatic change in England and America. Instead of being a matter of educated gentlemen producing a limited number of expensive copies of their learned writings for a small circle of like-minded subscribers, authorship took on the shape that we know today: that of a business designed to sell the largest possible number of mass-produced copies of a work for profit, to anyone who could be persuaded to buy. This phenomenon— the result of increased literacy and leisure in the general population, along with tremendous improvements and economies in book manufacture and distribution—was greeted with mixed feelings by the literary establishment in England. But in America the idea of a nation of readers accorded well with democratic aspirations. During Hawthorne's youth, therefore, the profession of authorship was being held out by cultural leaders as a way to achieve fame, fortune, and immense popularity while contributing to two important patriotic enterprises: enlightening the masses and establishing the United States as a nation of culture and taste.

But as a profit-making business, publishing was less a leader of the new masses of readers than a follower, for if people didn't expect to like a work, they wouldn't buy it. The most successful kinds of publication became the newspaper, the magazine, and fiction in any shape or form—types of writing that had never before been accorded high status.

Fiction, indeed, had always been despised and condemned by Puritan leaders, who saw it as dishonest and distracting; and it had also been dismissed as useless by such Enlightenment figures as Benjamin Franklin. Yet in the nineteenth century it appeared to observers that the American appetite for fiction had become simply insatiable. The transformation of fiction from a despised genre to the favorite reading of the day involved, among democratic Americans, a reassessment of its quality and value. As fiction became more popular, its prestige increased. From the historical novels of Sir Walter Scott in the 1810s and 1820s, through the comic and melodramatic social novels of Charles Dickens in the 1830s and 1840s, and then the ironic realism of William Makepeace Thackeray and the social protest fiction of Elizabeth Gaskell in the 1840s, novels (and fiction more generally) were increasingly accepted as major sources of knowledge and wisdom about human nature and society. For the first time, novelists were described as artists. But where was the American novelist to match the great British writers? In Hawthorne's youth only James Fenimore Cooper seemed even remotely a candidate for a place beside Scott or Dickens. A dreamy and ambitious young man, who loved fiction almost better than life, could indeed have fantasies of glory.

Nevertheless, American publishers, for all their grand talk, were not notably supportive of American writers. Since there was no international copyright, it was much cheaper for them to reprint books from abroad than to pay royalties to American authors. During the very years that many were loudly calling for a national literature, it seemed sometimes as if publishers were supplying American readers with works by writers of every nation except their own. Only a handful of highly popular writers managed, during Hawthorne's lifetime, to make a good living through their writing, and they did so by being extremely productive. The profession was not geared for authors who worked slowly and carefully, or whose creativity alternated with long periods of gestation.

Commonly, therefore, imaginative writers would augment their earnings through editing or magazine journalism, or by political appointments. The poet William Cullen Bryant, for example, was chief editor of the *New York Evening Post* for almost fifty years beginning in 1829; Edgar Allan Poe worked as reviewer and editor for more than a half dozen magazines in Charleston, Philadelphia, and New York City; James Fenimore Cooper was the United States consul at Lyons from 1826 to 1833; Washington Irving held diplomatic posts in Spain and England. And Nathaniel Hawthorne in his turn was to hold appointments at the Boston customhouse, the Salem customhouse, and as United States consul in Liverpool.

Hawthorne began his literary career writing short pieces, which he published anonymously in a variety of periodicals. "Secret" publication of this sort was quite usual, not because writing was an unacceptable profession, but because authors did not want their reputations tarnished by unpopular apprentice work. Not until their stories had received favorable notice did they come forward in their own names, as Hawthorne did when he collected tales and sketches in the 1837 volume *Twice-Told Tales*. As a steady but slow worker, he did not write a long piece of fiction before *The Scarlet Letter,* and although after that he planned to write long fiction only, he found that the toll on his energies was too great to sustain the pace of a novel every year or every other year. Thus, he had to abandon his hope of making a living from literature.

Appropriately, therefore, one can locate *The Scarlet Letter* in its day as Hawthorne's attempt to realize the possibilities of authorship in a country that accorded high status, but little support, to a professional writer; to blend the time-honored power of fiction to enchant and entertain with its newly recognized capacities for psychological and social analysis; and to contribute to the national life by providing, within the boundaries of a popular form, a thoughtful contemporary examination of the Puritan heritage. In his career it occupies a turning point: secure in his creative powers after a long apprenticeship, he turned from the safer, slighter short form to the challenges and rewards of the novel.

The publication of *The Scarlet Letter* inaugurated a period of considerable productivity for Hawthorne, with two more novels published in the next two years. *The House of the Seven Gables* (1851), set in his native Salem but incorporating many characteristic elements of the marvelous, dealt (as does *The Scarlet Letter* in a different fashion) with the long-term effects of crime and guilt on two families. *The Blithedale Romance* (1852) took place in a utopian community modeled on Brook Farm, chronicling the destruction of the reformers' dreams and ambitions by their own human shortcomings.

Hawthorne's acceptance of a consular appointment and his move to Europe had the unintended effect of terminating his literary career. The impact of Europe on his consciousness was exhilarating but also overwhelming, and consular duties along with sightseeing and family responsibilities absorbed all his energies. His last completed novel, *The Marble Faun* (1859), was another fantasy about guilt and crime, and their effects on history and the human psyche. It was set in Italy; its characters were young American and Italian artists.

When Hawthorne returned to the United States he felt displaced and alienated. He had grown accustomed to life in Europe and was made uncomfortable by the war atmosphere that had transformed American life. He began work on three different novels, two of them dealing with the return of an American of English descent to the old country, and one about a search for the "elixir of life," a drink that would confer immortality. Although his active literary career had essentially ceased in 1852, and although his only lukewarm support of the North during the Civil War alienated the critics, he was acclaimed on his death as America's foremost man of letters.

The Importance of The Scarlet Letter

When thinking about what we mean when we call a literary work a masterpiece, we should remember that ultimately such judgments do not have absolute or objective validity, but depend on a cultural consensus, usually elaborated by those who are specially trained, about what it means for literature to be "great." In one culture—to give a simple example—traces of individuality in a work might disqualify it for high praise; in another—notably our own, Western, modern culture—a literary work that cannot be identified as the creation of a specific author is immediately classified as the product of a "formula" and dismissed from consideration for masterwork status.

What we tend to require for something called a literary masterwork is: a display of great craftsmanship, indicating that the author has "mastered" the chosen medium, whether it is novel, short story, sonnet, ode, tragedy, or comedy; striking originality, which—almost paradoxically—transcends the rules of craft that the author has mastered; and clear traces of an individual sensibility in the work. Beyond this, and probably more important to us, the text must make a powerful emotional and intellectual impact, provide a rich reading experience, and leave behind a larger understanding of our past experience and perhaps a new way to think about our lives. In the case of the greatest works we return to them time and again in our minds, even if we do not reread them frequently, as touchstones by which we interpret the world around us. These conditions have been satisfied, for generations of readers, by *The Scarlet Letter*.

Literary skill. Every critic who has written about *The Scarlet Letter* has acknowledged that its plot is concisely elaborated in a structure that is virtually perfect in its pacing and symmetry; and that its style—more stately and less colloquial than is now the norm—displays a rich command of linguistic resources, including an extensive and precise vocabulary, diverse sentence structure, modulations in tone, and a striking variety of rhetorical devices ranging from attention to the sound of words on through complicated development of figures of speech, images, and symbols. To read *The Scarlet Letter* carefully is to gain an enlarged sense of what a true craftsman can do with language, and with the challenge of telling a story.

Originality. The story of *The Scarlet Letter* does not take long to tell, nor is its plot very complicated; but one does not have to read far into it to realize that its treatment of the aftermath of adultery is highly original; those familiar with literary history will know that it is unprecedented in its approach, and that it is extremely difficult to imitate. Those who are not experienced readers will recognize how unconventional the work is simply because of the surprises it puts in the way of reading, as the expected developments do not occur. Among its most original features are the development of characters who are partly realistic and partly stylized, and whose inner states of mind are considered far more important than their outer actions.

The traces of an individual sensibility. Once *The Scarlet Letter* has been read and absorbed, a reader can easily recognize other works by Hawthorne, can even identify individual sentences as the product of his hand. Not only the elaborate yet quiet style, but configuration of setting, situation, characters, and concerns in *The Scarlet Letter* are characteristic of this author and no other. Yet, individual elements can be extracted from the mixture and, when we see them in other writers, we call them "Hawthornian." In transcending genres Hawthorne invented his own genre.

Emotional and intellectual impact. The emotional impact of the novel rises from our engagement in the situation of the major characters, our appreciation of their dilemmas, and our reluctant acceptance of their destinies. In the interweaving of choice and fatality

Hawthorne's narrative approaches tragedy. The intellectual impact rises from the difficulty of assigning clear praise or blame to anyone, and the consequent necessity of working our way through the myriad implications and ramifications of the situation—the situation of each character taken separately, and the situation that all of them make together. This is why the book achieves so much depth with so small a cast of characters. The intellectual work that Hawthorne demands of us enlarges our understanding and distinguishes *The Scarlet Letter* from entertainment that leaves us unchanged, although of course if there were no entertainment in *The Scarlet Letter* Hawthorne would not have expected us to read it. Certainly part of the "craft" involved in a masterwork of fiction is the achievement of a satisfying piece of entertainment.

Touchstones for our lives. For hundreds of thousands of readers since 1850, the four important characters in *The Scarlet Letter*—Hester Prynne, Arthur Dimmesdale, Roger Chillingworth, and Pearl—have become part of their mental landscape. If they hear of an obsessively vengeful man, they will think of Chillingworth; a beautiful but wild child will remind them of Pearl; reading about a respected member of the community exposed for a secret sin, they will think of Dimmesdale; and finding themselves in conflict with authority, scorned by public opinion for doing what they believe to be right, they will identify themselves (whether they are men or women) with Hester Prynne. As for the symbol of the scarlet letter itself, it has achieved a kind of status as shorthand for any negative labeling imposed on an individual by his or her surroundings. A work that makes this kind of impact on our self-understanding cannot be anything but important.

Finally, readers usually expect American masterworks to tell them something about the country, or at least to reflect about the meaning of being an American. Typically, Hawthorne does not so much "tell us" about America as provide the framework within which certain questions may be raised and their answers attempted. His examination of Puritanism, of community authority, and of individualism in *The Scarlet Letter* touches on themes at the center of American history and American thought.

The Critical Reception

Many works thought to be literary classics in their time have disappeared from view while other works ignored in their day have resurfaced as classics in later times. *The Scarlet Letter* is one of the rare American literary works that, recognized as a "classic" at once, has also remained in print constantly from first appearance to the present.

In fact, it was recognized as a classic even before publication, when James T. Fields, one of the three partners in the firm that published Hawthorne's works, read the manuscript. It was he who persuaded the self-doubting author to allow him to publish it as a single separate work rather than in a mixed collection of short pieces, as had been Hawthorne's original intention. Field's enthusiasm was particularly striking in that the work was truly "defective" in just the way Hawthorne thought it was: it was not a mixture of bright and dark, sunshine and shadow, humor and pathos, as the taste of the time preferred. Rather, it was intense and single in its stress on the dark, the somber, the gloomy.

It is "positively a hell-fired story, into which I found it almost impossible to throw any cheering light," Hawthorne wrote to a close friend at the time that he finished the work. The sentence suggests that far from realizing his own intentions—which were to write something pleasing and popular, with plenty of variety—*The Scarlet Letter* had stubbornly gone its own way in the creation. Thus, when he read the conclusion to his wife, he was jubilant to discover how deeply it affected her. "It broke her heart and sent her to bed with a grievous headache—which I look upon as a triumphant success!" he wrote in the same letter. "Judging from its effect on her and the publisher, I may calculate on what bowlers call a ten-strike."

A "ten-strike" it was, so far as Hawthorne's reputation was concerned; for with the publication of *The Scarlet Letter* he was instantly elevated to the position of the nation's foremost man of letters. But the popularity that he greatly desired—for financial reasons and because he had always thought of writing as a way of establishing community with an audience—did not come with this or any other work. The book did not sell much over 13,500 copies between publication and Hawthorne's death thirteen years later; his total royalties amounted to little more than $1,500. Even allowing for the uninflated dollar, this sum cannot be regarded as a significant success. Hawthorne has owed his continuing reputation to the appreciation with which a small but influential audience has responded to his work, above all to *The Scarlet Letter*.

Such an audience had first come into being during the 1840s and was chiefly composed of literary critics who wrote for magazines and newspapers. They had appreciated his 1837 *Twice-Told Tales* enough to induce him to republish the work in an expanded edition in 1842; had approvingly read his new writings as they appeared in John L. O'Sullivan's *United States Magazine and Democratic Review* in the 1840s; and welcomed the 1846 collection *Mosses from an Old Manse*. These critics were hoping to find an American writer of fiction with a distinct national flavor, who was good enough to be proposed seriously as an equal to the great English and French novelists of the 1840s, among whom were Charles Dickens, William Makepeace Thackeray, Elizabeth Gaskell, Victor Hugo, and Alexandre Dumas. James Fenimore Cooper had fallen from favor because he had abandoned his popular Leatherstocking series and other historical subjects to write polemical novels strongly critical of American democracy. Catharine Sedgwick, who had been thought equal to Cooper as a historical novelist in the 1820s, had abandoned novel writing for didactic tracts. Edgar Allan Poe (who died in 1849) refused to write novels because he believed in the importance of a "unity of effect" that was only attainable in works that could be read in a single sitting. Herman Melville, a recent and promising arrival on the literary scene with *Typee* in 1846, had quickly become too wild and metaphysical for contemporary critical taste. *The Scarlet Letter* was not quite the kind of work that critics had been looking for, but they were prepared to be flexible if they could safely announce it as a major American novel.

In addition, a political scandal had broken around Hawthorne just before he began work on *The Scarlet Letter:* his patronage appointment at the Salem customhouse, which had been assured to him regardless of which party was in power, was terminated when the Whigs beat out the Democrats late in 1848. A highly respected literary man thus found himself unemployed, with a family to support, in 1849; and Hawthorne accompanied the text of *The Scarlet Letter* with a long prefatory essay (called "The Custom-House") that provided a satirical account of life in the customhouse as well as his dismissal. This topical material assured that the book would be well publicized, even though critics might concentrate on "The Custom-House" rather than *The Scarlet Letter;* it assured that reviews of the book would be widely read, and not only by people interested in literature. Some were ready to defend the author, others to defend his being fired. Some people approved of his putting his reactions into print, others thought it unseemly of him to have done so. But, in any event, "The Custom-House" gave Hawthorne wide publicity.

In fact, regardless of their political alignments, leading critics of the day generally reviewed *The Scarlet Letter* very favorably, concentrating on its stylistic and formal perfection, its intensity of effect, its insight into the human soul, its "pathos and power," its mixture of solemnity and tenderness, severity and sympathy. While they might have preferred a work of more humor and playfulness, they found in *The Scarlet Letter* a tragic essence worthy of a major writer, and happily ranked Hawthorne with leading nineteenth-century European authors. The hostile reviews came from critics with a strong religious orientation, who deemed the author's choice of subject—an adulterous couple—immoral in itself regardless of the author's treatment. Many of these thought, in addition, that Hawthorne had treated his sinners too sympathetically, in a manner likely to encourage similar immorality among readers.

Hawthorne's subsequent novels were compared as a matter of course with *The Scarlet Letter.* A number of critics preferred *The House of the Seven Gables.* So did Hawthorne, who wrote in a letter that it was "a more natural and healthy product of my mind," and that he "felt less reluctance in publishing it" than he did *The Scarlet Letter* because it was a more cheerful book with a more varied tone.

Over time, however, *The Scarlet Letter* came to be recognized as the best of his works, as well as the one that—notwithstanding Hawthorne's own self-analysis—most represented his literary methods and concerns.

In the decades after Hawthorne's death a group of prestigious Boston-based literary critics worked tirelessly to maintain his reputation as the foremost American writer. Once again certain extraneous factors were at work, chiefly the desire of these critics to develop a canon of national literature centering on New England writers. In the 1880s, when Houghton Mifflin, a Boston publishing company, began to put out elegant editions of the "major" American writers, Hawthorne was among the first to be featured. The success of this effort of critics and publishers can be measured by the fact that beginning with Henry James, whose long essay on Hawthorne appeared in 1879, numerous aspiring novelist-critics, including James, William Dean Howells, D. H. Lawrence, Jorge Luis Borges, and John Updike, have felt the need to engage with and write about Hawthorne's achievement. And every general critical study of American literature includes extended discussion of Hawthorne and *The Scarlet Letter*.

James described *The Scarlet Letter* as "the finest piece of imaginative writing yet put forth in the country." In assessing it, he took an approach often repeated in criticism through the years, identifying it as much with general New England culture as with the author's particular sensibility. "It belonged to the soil, to the air; it came out of the very heart of New England." While denying that the work was a historical novel in the normal sense—"the historical coloring is rather weak than otherwise; there is little elaboration of detail, of the modern realism of research"—James added that, nevertheless, Puritanism "is there, not only objectively, as Hawthorne had tried to place it there, but subjectively as well . . . in the very quality of his own vision." By "Puritanism" James did not imply any particular theology, but rather the intellectual, allegorical quality of the work, what he called "its element of cold and ingenious fantasy, its elaborate imaginative delicacy," which he attributed to the passionless reserve of Hawthorne's New England temperament.

During the last thirty years of the nineteenth century literary critics elaborated on an idea of fiction as inclining either to a realist or to a romantic practice, and Hawthorne came to figure as the ultimate romantic. The difference between these two modes was not in the choice of subject matter, which was assumed to be truths of human life, but in the relation between these truths and the imagined facts that constituted the fiction. The realist worked inductively, like a scientist, beginning with observed facts of life and working from them to his truths; the romantic worked deductively, in the reverse direction, beginning with certain truths and using the facts of his story to illustrate them. A distinction like this might explain why Hawthorne could lean so heavily on the fantastic, the supernatural, the symbolic, and the allegorical and yet create a sense of truth as strong as in any realistic novel.

Over time, and perhaps inaccurately, the tradition of American fiction came to be associated with romantic practice, which led to the institution of *The Scarlet Letter* as the very fountainhead of a truly American fiction. (This is an ironic development, since Hawthorne often claimed that his imagination was un-American in its preference for the romantic.) In its role as the quintessential American novel *The Scarlet Letter* was attacked as often as it was defended, for numerous important novelists of the later nineteenth century set themselves firmly in the realist camp, among them such important critics as William Dean Howells, a great admirer of Hawthorne who nevertheless regarded him as an influence to be overcome. But every essay that criticized *The Scarlet Letter* for excessive fantasy or lack of realism testified to its continuing and powerful presence on the literary horizon. *The Scarlet Letter* continues to be accepted without argument as an indisputable fictional masterwork of the pre–Civil War era, and this recognition underlies all criticism in the twentieth century.

Between the turn of the twentieth century and World War II much discussion of Hawthorne and *The Scarlet Letter* had a biographical emphasis, viewing the novel less in and for itself than as an index to the fascinating psyche of its author. Behind a variety of up-to-date psychological theories such criticism actually returned to the question that the earliest reviews had raised, the question that had so worried Hawthorne himself: whether the author and his works were excessively gloomy. The concern in *The Scarlet Letter* with the isolation of particular human beings from the larger society and the reasons for that isolation, as well as the focus on secrets and guilt, were taken as expressions of Hawthorne's personal maladjustment, and critics searched the biographical records for explanation. Some found it in the absent father who had died almost before Hawthorne could remember him; some in an allegedly eccentric and withdrawn mother; others in the foot injury that kept him from active play at a crucial time in his youth; others in the oppressive New England heritage.

Another group of critics dealt with Hawthorne's supposed morbidity by arguing that he was not in the least morbid, but was a well-balanced man in both his life and his works; still others maintained that the critical demand for cheer and balance was naive and narrow. A powerful way of accounting for the differing critical responses that a reading of *The Scarlet Letter* obviously produced was to stress Hawthorne's "ambiguity," that is, the way in which he makes it difficult or impossible to extract a clear and particular "message" from his work. Studies of the means by which such ambiguity was achieved became, in the 1950s, the chief way of investigating the text itself.

The upshot of such studies was a supplanting of the view of Hawthorne as romantic allegorist (since allegory is a technique for imposing single, clear meanings) with the idea of Hawthorne as symbolist. In line with such a change, critics grew less interested in Hawthorne's use of earlier sources (Milton, Spenser, John Bunyan, and the like) and more interested in his influence on later writers; where he had often been thought of as creating a deliberately archaic kind of fiction, he was now perceived in the opposite light: as the forerunner of various modern techniques. An important 1957 study by Charles Feidelson, *Symbolism and American Literature,* made this point especially strongly.

Some critics, accepting the notion of Hawthorne's personal isolation in life and its causative power in his work, attributed his situation to shortcomings in society rather than in the man. More specifically they pointed either to his dissent from the obligatory optimism of mid-nineteenth-century America, which required belief in progress and human perfectibility as articles of faith, or to his difficult situation as a "serious" artist in a society that loved trivia. In such interpretations, as "blame" shifts from Hawthorne to society, emphasis veers from the psychological to the sociological, and Hawthorne begins to be understood not as an explorer of general human truths, but as a social critic. This is probably the most important development in criticism of *The Scarlet Letter* in the last forty years, but it shares with the biographical criticism a desire to fold the particular work into a larger field of inquiry. The blending of an earlier idea of Hawthorne's "romantic" method in *The Scarlet Letter* with a later sense of his presumed social purpose received one of its strongest and most influential statements in Richard Chase's 1957 study, *The American Novel and Its Tradition*. This work had as its prime goal to establish a distinction between American and British fiction. Chase called *The Scarlet Letter* an allegorical novel whose "allegory both in form and substance derives from Puritanism" and whose theme is the "loss or submergence of emotion involved in the abandonment of the Old World cultural heritage."

Again, however, the characteristics of the work itself came into play because interpretations of *The Scarlet Letter* as social commentary could not escape the text's ambiguity any more than could the biographical criticism. Where one critic (e.g., Hyatt Waggoner in *Hawthorne: A Critical Study*) might present Hawthorne as an old-fashioned conservative who did not believe in human goodness, and who exploited Puritanism as a corrective to his age, another critic (e.g., D. H. Lawrence in *Studies in Classic American Literature*) might argue with equal force and passion that *The Scarlet Letter* was a profound although disguised attack on an emotionally impoverishing and hypocritical American moralism.

Hawthorne's ambiguity entered Chase's interpretation, too, in that Chase decided Hawthorne had not committed himself as to whether the loss of the Old World heritage was good or bad for Americans. Following Chase, any number of critics from Joel Porte (*The Romance in America*, 1969) to Michael Davitt Bell (*The Development of Amer-*

ican Romance, 1981) have interpreted *The Scarlet Letter* as a work whose form is particularly "American," whose point is to criticize society from an alienated perspective that reflects Hawthorne's personal and professional situation.

Along with the interest in assimilating *The Scarlet Letter* to more general inquiry, biographical and social criticism share an approach to the work as an entity to be "interpreted." This approach is strikingly different from that prevailing in Hawthorne's own time, where the work was considered in relation to its ability to engage reader emotions, not as a text encoding a message for the intellect to decipher. The many critics in the second half of the twentieth century who have restricted their view to "the text itself" have also shared this preoccupation with interpretation and have attempted to come up with a basic and correct "meaning" for *The Scarlet Letter.*

Two questions have especially preoccupied them. One is whether Hawthorne's worldview is essentially religious or secular, whether he thinks that his characters have "sinned" in the sense of breaking a divine commandment or whether, instead, he thinks they have broken a social law. A second, connected question is: which characters does Hawthorne sympathize with, and why? Answers to these questions vary widely; there are those who see Hester as an out-and-out secular heroine standing up for the individual against arbitrary authority, and those who see her as a religious sinner, adding pride and anger to her original trespass. Those who are committed to a secular reading of Hawthorne take *The Scarlet Letter* as a powerful psychological study of the inner life; those committed to a religious reading find its strength rather in Hawthorne's rejection of his characters' rationalizations, his adherence to an ethical absolutism based on belief in a firm divine order that takes precedence over human desire.

The fact that critics could come up with so many different, yet defensible, readings of *The Scarlet Letter* eventually led again to the matter of Hawthorne's ambiguity, but with a few new twists. Some contemporary critics now believe that ambiguity is inescapable in all linguistic texts; because language itself is inherently unstable (including the language in which critics make their arguments), no "interpretation" can ever be definitively established as the right one. Even those who prefer to think of language as more solid than this may agree that the world of a complex fictional text like *The Scarlet Letter* is bound to be so resonant and rich in connotations that different readers will necessarily have different responses. Some responses will be overly personal, and hence "unauthorized" by the text, but many will simply be based on sensitivities to different elements in the mixture. For example, in recent years feminist critics have turned to *The Scarlet Letter* because it is one of the few acknowledged American masterworks from before the Civil War whose main character is a woman. A feminist perspective allows one to see how Hawthorne was concerned, in developing Hester, with the question of the status of women in society, as well as the different commitments men and women tend to make to romantic love. Since romantic love serves Hester so badly, they can identify a previously unnoticed aspect of Hawthorne's social criticism: the idea of romantic love as a trick to ensure the willing subservience of women to the social system. This feminist perspective responds to elements truly there but completely invisible to those looking only for a theological statement in the novel.

Perhaps, then, the most exciting thing about *The Scarlet Letter* is not that we can translate it into a core meaning, but that it is full of meanings; though a dead work if it is not read, it comes to life for each reader in a slightly different way, just as human beings do for each other. The elusiveness of the text is thus the essential reason for its continuing fascination throughout the years. Unlike simpler works that are skimmed and discarded when we have extracted their "message" once and for all, *The Scarlet Letter* creates a world that we each enter in our own way, indeed that each of us may enter in different ways at different points in our lives. We do not surrender to an anarchistic subjectivity here; rather we recognize that interpretation is not the "last word" in an encounter with a great work of literature. If it were, we would never return to a masterpiece after we had learned its message, and it would have no capacity to move us after the first reading.

A

READING

1

WHAT?
THE STORY

When we begin to read a novel we enter an imaginary world created through words. If it works, the novel persuades us to accept that world on its own terms, for the duration of the reading, no matter how remote or farfetched that created world may be. This ability to lift us out of our surroundings is part of the immense attractiveness of narrative art. We leave the real world, more or less quickly, more or less comfortably, partly with the aid of conventions about fiction learned so long ago, and so often repeated, that they have come to seem perfectly natural. No "real world," for example, comes in numbered or titled chapters; yet a novel without them would seem unnatural. While depending on such shared conventions, however, each novel is also unique, and must instruct readers specifically in how to live in its world. Thus every good novel, whether a work of transient popularity or a would-be classic, tells us how it should be read, and never more intensely than in the opening pages. If it does not establish rapport with readers at the beginning, the novel may have no readers at the end.

THE SCARLET LETTER

ON THE THRESHOLD

In *The Scarlet Letter* a very brief opening section—one separate sentence, and two longish paragraphs—is set apart as a first chapter. Such emphasis, for an amount of prose that would normally be simply part of a longer chapter, says something about the pacing of the whole work: this novel will proceed deliberately, with pauses along the way. Indeed, in the first sentence we find ourselves present at a moment of arrest, as a crowd of people waits for something to happen, something to begin. If our fictional senses are keen, if we are inclined to let the book work its spell, we too will be put in a mood of anticipation. And we will ask: who are these people? where are we? It is through the implicit raising of questions, and the more or less delayed answering of them, that a story engages the attention and interest of its readers.

The first sentence does say something about where we are: it provides clues in the description of the people's clothing—"sad-colored garments and gray, steeple-crowned hats"—and in its reference to a "wooden edifice" and a door "heavily timbered with oak, and studded with iron spikes" (47). Men don't wear steeple-crowned hats any longer, nor are buildings made with doors like the one described. We are in the past; but was it the past to Hawthorne's contemporaries? Any doubts a reader of today might have about this are settled in the next paragraph, when the narrator refers to "the forefathers of Boston" and locates the action "some fifteen or twenty years after the settlement of the town." So we know that Hawthorne was addressing an audience that, like us, was not contemporaneous with the action of his story. *The Scarlet Letter* was never set in present time for any reader.

The first sentence goes beyond intimations about historical time and place and begins to tell us something about the *kind* of world we are in. It does this by mixing straightforward description with connotative terms that imply attitudes. It uses the phrase "sad-colored" rather than giving us a list of colors. The impression created by the term is intensified by the description of the door: heavily timbered, studded with iron spikes. Even this early in the story we recognize an atmosphere of sadness, of oppression, of antagonism. And we recognize that we must read not only for historical detail, but also for mood and atmosphere; perhaps the mood and atmosphere will be even more informative than the detail.

The atmosphere continues to build in the next sentence, which begins the second paragraph of this brief chapter: "The founders of a new colony, whatever Utopia of human virtue and happiness they might originally project, have invariably recognized it among their earliest practical necessities to allot a portion of the virgin soil as a cemetery, and another portion as the site of a prison" (47). This one sentence, placed where it is, performs a number of tasks. It tells us immediately that we are in a new colony, founded for some utopian purpose (and even if we did not know what a "utopia" was, we could conclude from the terms "virtue" and "happiness" that the colony had been founded for idealistic reasons). But in this colony, like all others (says the narrator), certain inescapable realities have manifested themselves very early on. Death and crime, the antithesis of happiness and virtue, have forced the founders—unless they were a particularly "realistic" group of idealists—to modify their plans. At once, then, it puts in question the possibility of all utopias, and suggests that the "story" of *The Scarlet Letter* may be about things going wrong in a projected utopia. Such an interpretive frame is not inherent in the historical setting itself; it is created by the connotative words in which the setting is conveyed.

The reader can also recognize a change in narrative procedure from the first to the second sentence of "The Prison-Door." The first sentence, though it contains some words suggesting an interpretation of the scene, is mainly expository—descriptive—in its nature. The second reverses the emphasis; it contains some exposition, but consists mostly of interpretive commentary. Thus, we recognize that this narration will move freely in and out of the action, will supplement the action with various kinds of commentary ranging from opinion on the specific action all the way to large-scale generalizations about universals. The action, apparently, will be strongly mediated by commentary provided by a narrator who, rather than concealing himself, will regularly stress his presence.

Why should a writer create so prominent a narrator? Isn't it better for the reader, and a sign of more skill in the writer, if stories appear to tell themselves? It was conventional for the novel of Hawthorne's time to have narrators who conversed freely with their readers. Through such narrators the novel-reading experience was presented as though it were a storytelling experience, where the storyteller, though not a character in the action, is a crucial figure in the narrative transaction. But Hawthorne may have had particular reasons for deploying a highly visible narrator in *The Scarlet Letter,* reasons that made it wise to establish the narrator's presence as quickly as possible. First, the time period and culture of his story may have already become quite distant to his audience, requiring a good deal of explanation to make these comprehensible. Second, the story that he wants to tell may have been sufficiently unconventional to call for extra help in making sure that the readers knew how to respond.

In just two sentences Hawthorne has conveyed a greal deal about what readers are to expect in *The Scarlet Letter,* and thus how they are to read it. Reflecting on how much Hawthorne has packed into the sentences, we may suppose that *The Scarlet Letter* is going to be a compressed work with a greal deal going on all the time. This is not a long book to be dipped into, but a short one to be unpacked word by word. And it is not to be read for the action alone, but also for the implications and resonances—the narrative embroidering, so to speak—of that action.

The second paragraph goes on to specify the setting in more detail. The "new colony" is Boston, about twenty years after it was settled (the colony was established in 1630). We read the names Cornhill, Isaac Johnson, King's Chapel. For most of us these allusions cannot do more than supply the impression of accuracy, encouraging a belief that the narrator is well informed. We would prefer to take a historical guided tour from a trustworthy person, and a few such specific references inspire the requisite confidence. (Too many of them might produce boredom, or a confused sense that we are not reading a novel after all.) Scholarly research has indicated, by the way, that Hawthorne did turn to historical sources for information of this sort, even though he does not always follow them. The references to the layout of early Boston are correct.

The paragraph also goes on to imply more about the action to come, and continues its work of creating an interpretive perspective through which the action is to be viewed. The building we stand in front of is a prison. Why would people have assembled in front of a prison door? For no other reason than to see the door open, which means to see someone come out. So we know that the story is about someone who has been put in prison. We wonder who, we wonder why, and we wonder for what reason the person is coming out. And—since we know that stories always have conflict—we sense the outlines of a conflict, between the person in the prison and those others, assembled outside the door. Now a crucial story question comes up; whose side are we on? For a story—this we know from the conventions of story-telling that have become natural to us—always has an actor who is the focus of audience sympathy. It is usual for the focus of sympathy to be the person whom the story is "about," and we already know that the story is about the soon-to-emerge criminal. Although it would seem natural, since an audience probably consists in the main of law-abiding citizens, for sympathies to be against the "criminal," a number of strategies in the paragraph prevent this "natural" flow of sympathies from occurring.

For one thing, there is the crowd. In its sad-colored clothing and its stony silence it does not invite reader sympathy. For another, there is the prison itself, especially the door. The prison and the door are described in such forbidding terms that a reader can hardly avoid beginning to feel sympathy for the unknown prisoner. They are dark, gloomy, old, heavy, oppressive, hostile, ugly. The descriptive words, by association and contiguity, seem to refer out and back to the crowd; crowd and prison become one; we sense a world unified in hostility to this prisoner. An impulse of fairness creates the inclination to support the prisoner, if only to weight the balance a little more evenly.

But Hawthorne—or the narrator (whichever term one prefers to use)—does not leave the creation of sympathy entirely to an assumed audience instinct for fair play, or to a dislike for ugly buildings and drab crowds. He goes quite far in his elaboration of the building's unsightliness, moving from its ugly architecture to the equally unappealing vegetation growing around it. Then, there rises from this vegetable imagery the first of what will turn out to be almost countless metaphors and similes, as the prison itself becomes a plant, the "black flower of civilized society" (48). Well, what do we think of a "black flower"? It is ugly, it is unnatural (there are no black flowers in nature), it is evil. Here we see a subtle confusion introduced: which is evil—the prison, or the crimes that have necessitated it?

We now see that this narrator, as well as interrupting his story for various sorts of commentary, is given to elaborating his narrative through images and metaphors. Such metaphors are more than literary decoration; they carry a good deal of information about the story. We are not surprised, then, when the metaphoric mode continues, and we discover that beside the prison door there grows "a wild rose-bush, covered, in this month of June, with its delicate gems," and that this wild rose bush is to be interpreted as a token of nature's sympathy with the prisoner.

In the contrast of the wild rose bush, with its flowers turned (by adding a second metaphor to the first) into gems, and the prison, turned metaphorically into an unnatural flower—the black flower of civilization—Hawthorne sets his conflict between prisoner and prison (or prisoner and crowd) into a much larger context. The rose bush is beautiful, also wild and natural; the black flower is ugly, also civilized and unnatural. Nature (personified—another kind of rhetorical device) has a heart to pity and be kind; civilization, apparently, does not. Is Hawthorne "saying" that civilization is unnatural, hence bad? Not necessarily; his work at this point is to create a frame within which we will feel sympathy for the prisoner, against what might be our "natural" impulses to feel antagonistic toward a criminal. What better way to do this than to associate the prisoner with the natural and the beautiful?

An especially perceptive reader, even a reader (if this were possible) coming to *The Scarlet Letter* with no prior information about its story whatsoever, might begin to think that the prisoner could, maybe, be a woman. The association of flowers and gems, youth and beauty, with the prisoner sets up this dim possibility, as does the adjective "fragile." The possibility quickly becomes probable when the rose bush is linked with one particular historical prisoner who happened to be a woman. Women criminals are sufficiently rare as to pique our curiosity; and the imbalance Hawthorne has been creating between the power of the community and the power of the prisoner is greatly intensified if the prisoner is female.

Anne Hutchinson—the "sainted" Anne Hutchinson, as the narrator describes her—is no "ordinary" woman criminal. We can let references to Cornhill and Isaac Johnson go by, perhaps; but Anne Hutchinson is so important a figure in early Puritan history that we can assume Hawthorne expected his readers to know something about her. Hutchinson had migrated with her husband to Boston in 1634. A brilliant and a kind woman, she was one of the few women religious leaders of the age, although of course she had no "official" status in a society that did not allow women to be magistrates or ministers, or to hold any kind of public office. At first her home was an important center for informal religious discussions but, rather quickly, she fell out of favor with the Puritan leaders.

There were two reasons for this. First, the Puritans had come to New England, not to practice religious tolerance, but to create their own theocracy, a society organized according to what they believed to be God's commands. In such a society absolute orthodoxy was a necessity, and in fact the Puritans became a tolerant people only much later in history than the time of *The Scarlet Letter*, only when so many non-Puritans had settled around them that they had no choice. They saw the intellectual position that Hutchinson developed as a kind of heresy. The name of her heresy (and it goes back to earliest Christianity) is antinomianism, and it consists of the doctrine that Christians are not bound by the moral law. Regeneration and salvation—the most serious issues to Puritan Christians—were inner matters with which external laws had nothing to do. Since the first generation of

Puritan leaders was certain that Puritan laws coincided with divine commandments, Hutchinson's views were completely unacceptable to them.

The second reason for opposition was that her preachings threatened the state in several ways. To begin with, the Puritan leaders did not like to see a woman step so far out of her supposedly God-given place as subordinate to men. And they had doctrinal concerns as well. A position that is indifferent, if not opposed, to law certainly undermines a society to which laws are essential. Too, although the Puritans strongly encouraged independent reading and study of the Bible, they saw Hutchinson and her large following as the nucleus of a state within a state, an alternative to the government they were constructing. This view was certainly enhanced by her claim to know who, among the colonists, was saved and who damned. The upshot was that Hutchinson was imprisoned, tried, instructed to recant (she did not), and in 1638 expelled from Massachusetts Bay. She went first to Rhode Island, and then to New York, where, in the winter of 1643, she and her family were killed by Indians—an event that the Puritans saw as divine retribution and confirmation of her errors.

Obviously a reference to such a prisoner as Anne Hutchinson greatly intensifies the aura of conflict between those who enforce the law and those who break it, simply because Hutchinson denied that law had any role to play where the soul was concerned. Carried a step further, Hutchinson's position can be seen to imply that "right" isn't necessarily, but may be, on the side of those who break the law. The law has judged the criminal, but who judges the law? Is Hawthorne saying that criminals are right? Not necessarily—but he does seem to be allowing for the possibility that they may not be wrong. And such a possibility allows us to sympathize with the still-unknown prisoner without feeling guilty of breaking a law ourselves.

What, then, of the word *sainted* referring to Anne Hutchinson? Doesn't that clearly show where the narrator's sympathies are? Perhaps. *Saint* is a word that the Puritans used with a special meaning, to refer to a person thought to be one of the elect, chosen by God to be saved (the Puritans emphatically did *not* believe in salvation available to all); the word could be used during a person's lifetime. If employed in accord with Puritan usage, "sainted" in this paragraph could represent Hutchinson's word for herself, or her claim to be "sainted" whether she followed the law or not, or the view of her held by some members of the community. It is, so to speak, a free-floating word not definitely attached to the narrator's own voice; or, if the narrator is using it in his own voice, he might be using it ironically. Here, then, we meet another crucial aspect of Hawthorne's method, spoken of by literary critics as his "ambiguity."

This term is used to refer to the immense difficulty one has when trying to find out exactly where he—the human author—stands on a particular moral or philosophical issue because his words are capable of being understood in two or more ways. In part, the extreme compression of Hawthorne's method creates ambiguity as a by-product; but, in part, the ambiguity cannot be other than intentional. For observe that not only does Hawthorne use the word *sainted* ambiguously; his linking of the rose bush with Hutchinson is only one explanation offered for how the bush came to be where it is. It might have merely survived, but it might have sprung up under her footsteps because she was "sainted." This is the first of many instances of the technique of alternative explanations in *The Scarlet Letter*. The purpose of such a technique is obviously to introduce multiple possibilities and hence to keep meaning open.

So our desire to find out exactly what Hawthorne means and where he stands may be misguided, or at any rate it may be thwarted. Intellectually, morally, and philosophically, Hawthorne keeps his options—and ours—open; but so far as story values are concerned, we have no choice but to take the emerging criminal, whoever she may be, as the character who is meant to engage our sympathies. Any lingering doubt we might have on this point cannot survive Hawthorne's final gesture, which is to pluck a flower from his metaphorical rose bush and offer it to us, the readers, as the "symbol of some sweet moral blossom" that we may find along the track of the story. The last two sentences of the chapter redirect our attention from the story proper back to its status as a work of written fiction. The direct address to the reader;

the placing not only of the criminal, but of the narrative itself, on the threshold of the prison door ("the threshold of our narrative, which is now about to issue from that inauspicious portal"); the reference to a "tale of human frailty and sorrow" (48)—all these remind us that a novel is not real, not life itself, but a special cultural act requiring cooperation between reader and narrator if it is to be successfully negotiated. Without such cooperation the narrative cannot get out of its prison. The narrator appeals to our sympathies, then, not only on behalf of the prisoner, but on behalf of *The Scarlet Letter* itself.

A STORY BEGINS

"The Prison-Door" has prepared us for a plot centered in a conflict between the Puritan settlement and an individual—most likely a woman—whom it has decreed a criminal. It has also suggested that the focus of the action may well come to be the question of whether this individual is really a criminal or not. But a framework is not a story; we still need specifics: particular events and particular agents to act and be acted upon. The plot begins in chapter 2, "The Market-Place," which particularizes the action within the terms that "The Prison-Door" has created. Throughout the chapter rhetorical and metaphorical contrasts between the lawgiving social body and the errant individual continue.

"The Market-Place" opens by returning us to the scene of the first sentence of "The Prison-Door," essentially reiterating the content of that sentence. "The grass-plot before the jail, in Prison Lane, on a certain summer morning, not less than two centuries ago, was occupied by a pretty large number of the inhabitants of Boston; all with their eyes intently fastened on the iron-clamped oaken door" (49). In the course of the next several pages the Puritans are repeatedly and emphatically characterized in terms that must deprive them of reader sympathy: their faces are "petrified" in a "grim rigidity"; their character is marked by "severity" and "solemnity"; their sympathies are "meagre" and "cold." The women in the crowd are "hard-featured," "self-constituted judges," "iron-visaged," "unkindly-visaged"; the men are "stern-browed"; and their entire system is aptly personified by the town beadle (the official whose business is to administer the law), who emerges from the prison "like a black shadow," his "grim and grisly presence" representing "the whole dismal severity of the Puritanic code of law" (52).

As part of the strategy of generating sympathy for Hester by creating reader antipathy toward the Puritan community, Hawthorne postpones her entrance until he has shown the opinions held of her by a chorus of women spectators. Through their talk we are informed that the criminal is indeed (as we suspected) a woman, that her name is Hester Prynne, that her punishment involves some kind of marking that she must wear on the bosom of her gown. As the women serve as an indirect channel of information, their manner of talking about her sets us against them. They are dismayed by what they interpret as the magistrates' leniency; they compete to suggest punishments of ever greater severity, culminating in the judgment that "this woman has brought shame upon us all, and ought to die." If the law is not applied to its fullest extent, says "the ugliest as well as the most pitiless" of these women, "let the magistrates, who have made it of no effect, thank themselves if their own wives and daughters go astray" (51–52).

The women—except for one, the only one who expresses sympathy for Hester—are old, ugly, and pitiless, and though age and ugliness are not crimes, there is no doubt that such characteristics make the women seem witchlike, resembling antagonists of moral virtue more than representatives of rectitude. Their inhumanity is made clearer by the contrast within the group between these hard-featured women and the compassionate young mother. Their conversation makes clear that Hester's has been a sin especially connected with their sex, that, in short, it has been a sexual sin. (Their talk also introduces Dimmesdale's name; an exceedingly clever reader will suspect—since the story is obviously not going to have a large cast of characters—that "Reverend Master Dimmesdale, her godly pastor" may have a role to play in the action.)

Now, finally (though in fact no later than the sixth page of the text, so economical has Hawthorne been in his preparations), the malefactor is allowed to make her entrance. Her first gesture epitomizes the conflict between herself and the settlement, and in this sense it is the true beginning of the story. On the threshold of the prison she shakes off the beadle's arm—"she repelled him, by an action marked with natural dignity and force of character, and stepped into the open air, as if by her own free–will" (52). The community is strong through law and might; she is strong through character. She has no choice but to accept her punishment, but will do so as if by her own free will. Within the boundaries of the possible Hester will strive to make her character felt; and since the purpose of the (as yet undescribed) mark is to efface her character, to make her subservient to the Puritan system, a struggle between Hester and the system is immediately established. And with it, two questions: who will win this battle? and how?

Moreover, there is no doubt that the manner in which Hester is depicted identifies her as a heroine. Physically, she is a beauty: tall, with a figure of perfect elegance, glossy hair, a marked brow and deep black eyes, ladylike, characterized by stateliness and dignity. Her beauty shines out, even in her misfortune. And one cannot help but admire the courage with which she faces the crowd, moving along "with a burning blush"—which shows that she feels her situation keenly, is not insensitive—"and yet a haughty smile, and a glance that would not be abashed" (52–53). This is not, we recognize, a character so weak as to be destroyed by what has happened to her, nor yet so dense as to be unaffected by it.

To call Hester a heroine is not to claim that she has no faults. A character with no defects tends to be uninteresting, and an uninteresting character cannot long be acceptable as a hero or heroine. In addition, perfection—since we know full well that it doesn't exist in real life—often takes an odd turn in fiction, with the "perfect" character increasingly appearing to be self-righteous, cold, or even hypocritical. In fact, this is just what seems to be happening with the Puritans; their certainty that they are "right" makes them less attractive than they would be if they had some doubts. Thus, a degree of faultiness in

Hester, far from disqualifying her from a heroine's role, makes her more suitable for it.

Can we see any fault in Hester at the beginning? Well, she *has* had an illegitimate child, and even in our far more emancipated age such behavior, though it may not be considered blameworthy, is seldom viewed as an occasion for praise. In Hawthorne's nineteenth century sex outside of marriage was, though not a criminal act, still generally accepted as a sign of moral defect, and the nineteenth-century narrator is careful not to praise Hester, even when he suggests that a Catholic might have been reminded of divine maternity by the spectacle of Hester and her child. Here, in contrast to the "sacred image of sinless motherhood" that Mary offers, "there was the taint of deepest sin in the most sacred quality of human life, working such effect, that the world was only the darker for this woman's beauty, and the more lost for the infant that she had borne" (56).

At the point at which she is introduced Hester's background is unknown. Following Hester's fantasies and memories as she stands on the scaffold, Hawthorne gives us enough of her past to let us understand her fall, but though this history may explain or even excuse her behavior, it does not necessarily make the behavior "good." If Hawthorne invites us to judge Hester's judges, such an invitation does not logically require us to accept her own self-judgment. Extenuating circumstances may extenuate, but they do not excuse. The key question for a twentieth-century person at this point, trying to understand how to take this story, is whether sexual activity should come under any sort of moral or criminal judgment at all. In *The Scarlet Letter* the answer to this question is not clear. What we can say is that, in choosing to put his story back in Puritan times, when all activity was self-evidently thought to have a moral dimension and to call for social judgment, he has allowed the question to be opened.

Hester comes from a family of "antique gentility," which has fallen on hard times—the "paternal home" is a "decayed house of gray stone, with a poverty-stricken aspect." Full of girlish beauty and healthy glow—a normally sexed individual (Hawthorne does not share the nineteenth-century view that holds that women should have no sexual feeling)—she married "a man well stricken in years" of "a pale, thin, scholar-like visage, with eyes dim and bleared," who "was slightly deformed" and with whom her life was "like a tuft of green moss on a crumbling wall" (58). In other words, because of her family's poverty, Hester had made an unsuitable marriage, which gave her neither emotional nor sexual satisfaction. This history leads inevitably, Hawthorne suggests, to her present situation. Even the magistrates accept this much, we find out in chapter 3 ("This woman is youthful and fair, and doubtless was strongly tempted to her fall" [63]).

I have said that the action of the story begins with Hester's gesture in repelling the beadle's arm. In one sense it may be thought of as having begun about a year earlier, with the commission of the deed that has set the settlement against her, the act of illicit sexual intercourse that has had its visible result in "a child, a baby of some three months old, who winked and turned aside its little face from the too vivid light of day" (52). To the extent that a fictional action begins when a system of harmony or at least equilibrium is disrupted, this prior, unnarrated act marks the beginning. And Hawthorne is thus starting his tale proper "in medias res," as the phrase goes—in the middle of things. In another sense, however, by putting the precipitating cause of the action outside of the story proper, Hawthorne makes clear that his interest is—and ours should be—less in the deed than in its repercussions. This means also that his interest is less in the physical experience than in its emotional, mental, and moral aspects. The beginning of the story in *this* sense would be neither the sex act nor Hester's rebuff of the beadle, but the birth of Pearl, who is the undeniable sign of the act. Thus, Hawthorne has introduced another question about the law: is it the act, or the sign of the act, that matters? If we commit a crime that nobody knows about, does it matter? It is most interesting that the community's way of responding to the "sign" of Hester's crime is by labeling her with another sign, the letter.

Along with Hester and the people, Hawthorne introduces us briefly to Pearl and dwells at length on the object for which his book is named, the scarlet letter. In his presentation of the letter we understand how it can become the heart of the conflict between Hester and

the Puritans, and how it can come to absorb the rich texture of meaning that Hawthorne will eventually attach to it. Amid the general
drabness and gloom of the scene as he has depicted it (notwithstanding
that it is a summer morning and the sun is shining brightly) the letter
is a strikingly exotic object, made of "fine red cloth, surrounded with
an elaborate embroidery and fantastic flourishes of gold thread," done
with enormous artistry, showing "fertility and gorgeous luxuriance of
fancy" on the part of its creator (53). It sets Hester completely apart
from the rest of the community, taking "her out of the ordinary relations with humanity, and inclosing her in a sphere by herself" (54)—
changing her from a human being to a symbol.

But, certainly, such a gorgeous letter is not what the magistrates had
in mind when they sentenced her to wear it, as the chorus of women
quickly makes clear. "Why, gossips, what is it but to laugh in the faces
of our godly magistrates, and make a pride out of what they, worthy
gentlemen, meant for a punishment?" (54). New terms—gorgeous,
luxuriousness, artistry, fancy—enter to make a new contrast between
Hester and the Puritans, and provide a new context for thinking about
what she has done and what they think of it. In terms of plot, we see
the initiation of a struggle for what we may call the "meaning" of the
letter—is it a punishment, as the magistrates planned it to be, or a
"pride"—something to be ashamed of, or something to be proud of?
The question of how we are to assess what Hester did becomes equivalent to the question of how we are to interpret the letter. So our
earlier questions—who will win this battle, and how?—become these:
whose "reading" of the letter will win, and how will that victory be
achieved? Since the community is stronger than the individual, the
community is more likely to win; but since we want the main character to win, and since Hester clearly is a person of unusual strength,
we think—we hope—that she has a chance. We know, at least, what
her victory would be: it would consist in forcing the community to
admit that they have misjudged her. A romantic reader—of which
there must be many in any novel audience—might hope that the victory would consist in her taking the letter off entirely. As we shall see,
Hawthorne is planning to take account of this hope.

THE SCARLET LETTER

THE PLOT THICKENS

The story and interest of *The Scarlet Letter* are both enhanced in chapter 3, "The Recognition," by the introduction of two new characters and the new plot elements associated with them. Up to now the conflict has been only between the prisoner and the imprisoners, Hester and the Puritans. This conflict is carried forward in "The Recognition" when we meet some of the officials of the settlement—the lawmakers, rather than the law-abiders—in action. From this point on the Puritan people (women) fade into the background, and the settlement is represented by those who have shaped its character, those in power, the authorities, who are, of course, men.

The leadership of the colony is epitomized by two figures, one political and one ecclesiastical, whose near association acts out Hawthorne's statement that these are "a people amongst whom religion and law were almost identical" (50), for whom "the forms of authority were felt to possess the sacredness of divine institutions" (64). The political figure is Richard Bellingham, identified as the governor of the colony (actually, the historical Bellingham's terms as governor of Massachusetts do not fit Hawthorne's time scheme), and John Wilson, called the eldest clergyman of Boston (although, again, in point of historical fact he was in his fifties during the decade when the action of this novel takes place). Without troubling ourselves unduly about why Hawthorne chose these two figures out of the range of historical possibilities, we can say that the economy of his story demanded a minimum use of characters with the greatest efficiency, and that he therefore settled on one representative for each of the two branches of the Puritan oligarchy.

And what does Hawthorne have to say of their abilities to judge Hester? "Out of the whole human family, it would not have been easy to select the same number of wise and virtuous persons, who should be less capable of sitting in judgment on an erring woman's heart, and disentangling its mesh of good and evil, than the sages of rigid aspect towards whom Hester Prynne now turned her face" (64). As usual, Hawthorne does not go so far as to say that Hester is without blame—

she is an "erring" woman, her heart a "mesh of good and evil"—but he again invites us to judge her judges.

Bellingham and Wilson give a focus to the previously undifferentiated mass of the Puritan crowd; these are the men who judge and punish Hester. Before we meet them, however, we have also found out that Hester's husband is, unknown to everybody except Hester herself, on the scene; and we quickly learn what complication his arrival portends. It turns out that the father of Hester's child is not known to the community and that she has steadfastly refused to name him. The anonymous husband makes clear that his business will be to identify the father: "It irks me, nevertheless, that the partner of her iniquity should not, at least, stand on the scaffold by her side. But he will be known!—he will be known!—he will be known!" (63). The complication is thus a second focus of struggle between Hester and the community—they want her to name the father and she resists—which is expanded into a struggle between Hester and her husband. Rather strikingly (and in all probability quite inaccurately, as a historical representation of Puritan procedure), the chief topic of the public dialogue between Hester and the magistrates is the identity of the unknown lover.

Perhaps needless to say at this point, Hester's concealment of his name helps to increase reader esteem for her. It shows her courageously standing up, even at the moment of her greatest humiliation, against the magistrates. It shows clearly that her misdeed proceeded from love that is not selfish ("And would that I might endure his agony, as well as mine!" [68]). And it opens a whole new field in which to consider Hester: it puts her in contrast with the unknown lover who is escaping exposure and punishment for doing the same thing that Hester did.

This unknown lover, to be sure, is not unknown to us. Certainly long before the chapter is over we know that it is Dimmesdale. Perhaps we know it as soon as a member of the crowd names him for the second time ("she hath raised a great scandal, I promise you, in godly Master Dimmesdale's church" [61]). For our grasp of Hawthorne's techniques leads us to see that in a story with so restricted a field of characters, he would not possibly give so much space to Dimmesdale if he were not an important character. And there is only one part that is unfilled. Again, the idea that Hester's lover should be a clergyman so clearly fits into the issues that Hawthorne has raised that the choice seems inevitable. Why not make a lawmaker and a lawbreaker one person? The continual references throughout the chapter to Dimmesdale's responsibility, as her minister, for Hester's soul, become deeply ironic.

Now, too, we have a second plot line as well as a complication of Hester's plot, a line that turns on the question—not of the identity of the lover, which we know—but on the exposure of that identity. Hester knows who he is, but will not speak. Dimmesdale knows who he is, but also will not speak. The Puritan community is completely taken in by his apparent purity. The husband, a man of learning, whose eyes have "a strange, penetrating power, when it was their owner's purpose to read the human soul" (58), will try to discover that identity.

Do we readers want the identity exposed? Certainly, a moral sense of justice and an aesthetic sense of symmetry would alike seem to call for it. Hester is humiliated and isolated on the pillory; Dimmesdale is aloft on the meetinghouse balcony, secure in the regard and esteem of the entire community. It does not seem fair. Hester, the scorned woman, carries the burden of her shame and his guilt and protects him out of love; Dimmesdale, the community idol, keeps his secret and preaches at her.

His "sermon" asking her to name her lover is a masterpiece of double-talk, urging her to provide the name if she thinks it will be good for her own soul's peace to do so (when, clearly, she would be full of self-hatred if she gave him away), while making clear to her that if she does not tell, he certainly will not, since he lacks the courage to face exposure. In terms of the logic of the story, there is only one way that the lover's identity can "properly" come out, and that is for Dimmesdale to disclose it himself. The ending of the story, that is to say—if justice is to prevail—calls for a situation where the relative positions of Hester and Dimmesdale in the community have been reversed: where he will be "marked," and she exonerated.

PLOT AND STRUCTURE

By the end of the first three chapters of *The Scarlet Letter*—together they take up less than a tenth of the novel—Hawthorne has begun an action, complicated it, brought all the characters on stage, established relationships between and among them, and provided a frame of metaphor and commentary within which to understand and evaluate what is taking place. All of this has been accomplished in what is, from a dramatic point of view, the novel's first scene—that is, within the confines of a single dramatized action.

A stage designer could place the prison on one side of the stage and the scaffold on the other without unduly distorting Hawthorne's spatial instructions: "it was no great distance, in those days, from the prison-door to the market-place" (55). Better still, cinema, with its ability to dissolve the boundaries between the inner and outer worlds, could follow Hawthorne's shifting points of view, beginning with a long shot of the crowd, zooming in on Hester and her scarlet letter, then adopting her perspective as she makes her journey to the pillory, which, "measured by the prisoner's experience . . . might be reckoned a journey of some length" (55), and finally, moving inside her consciousness to show her memories in a series of overlapping and shifting images. Neither film nor play can replicate the crucial role of the narrator, but to approach *The Scarlet Letter* as a scenario helps to abstract its narrative skeleton.

Chapter 4, "The Interview," is a separate scene but the contiguity of time and place to the first scene suggests its connection to chapters 1–3. Among other things, "The Recognition" has implied that there must be a meeting between Hester and her husband, and in "The Interview" this meeting takes place. After this chapter there is a break in the action, establishing the first four chapters as a unit.

The chapter gives the husband a name (although of course Roger Chillingworth is an assumed name) and a profession. The meeting of Hester and Roger shows the two coming to an accord with each other; or, more accurately, it shows Chillingworth announcing that "between thee and me, the scale hangs fairly balanced" (75). This easy mutual forgiveness has its roots in indifference. Hester has never loved Chillingworth and evidently any love he might ever have felt for her exists no longer. (It was, we might say, a purely selfish love.) But Chillingworth's interest in knowing the identity of the lover is intensely reiterated: "I shall seek this man, as I have sought truth in books; as I have sought gold in alchemy. . . . Thou wilt not reveal his name? Not the less he is mine" (75). And—this is the action needed to keep the plot moving—he makes Hester swear that she will keep his identity secret, above all secret from the father of her child.

Apparently Hester does not understand his purposes; she still thinks of him in connection with *her.* She hesitates, asking: "why not announce thyself openly, and cast me off at once?" (76). Chillingworth's equivocating answer makes clear that she and her child are not the reason, and he goes on to suggest that his motives are none of her business. "Enough, it is my purpose to live and die unknown" (76). Pressured both by her sense of duty to Chillingworth and by his threats of harm to the lover, in a distressed and exhausted mental state, Hester takes the oath even though she feels it to be wrong.

And the oath is a mistake. Chillingworth is now free to stay in Boston and attempt to solve the "mystery," as he calls it, of the lover's identity. In exchange, he has had to give up his own original identity, which, within the frame of this novel, is that of Hester's husband. To abandon an identity is, in a sense, to die, and Chillingworth's words make clear that this has happened to him: "Let, therefore, thy husband be to the world as one already dead, and of whom no tidings shall ever come" (76). The differences between Chillingworth's old identity and his new one are that in his old character he was in connection, however imperfectly, with love and warmth; he was required, however partially, to modify his behavior by reference to the behavior of others. Images of the household fire and its warmth characterize his description of their married life. His new identity denies him all possibility of human connection and frees him from all responsibility to other human beings. He is now accountable only to his own obsession.

Here, then, we have a second instance of a person denying the va-

lidity of the moral law where he is concerned, giving himself over to
the motives of his own heart. If, for any number of reasons, including
her attractiveness as well as our own personal susceptibility to strongly felt romantic love, we are inclined to justify a character like Hester,
hence to take an antinomian position ourselves, what are we to do
when the same kind of behavior, implying the same ethical stance, is
adopted by a character like Chillingworth?

For thematic purposes, then, Hester's oath makes Chillingworth
into a kind of double of Hester, while for plotting purposes it pits him
against her, since his aim is to discover the identity of the lover and
hers is to conceal it. In plot terms, therefore, Hester and Chillingworth
are adversaries in a struggle whose object is Dimmesdale. We must
anticipate another meeting between them.

And, since we are talking now of meetings, what about one between
Hester and Dimmesdale? Where, indeed, is the love story that propels
most novels? In a fascinating, low-key way *The Scarlet Letter* continually reminds us of the love story that it is *not*. Our very expectation
that novels will be about love and romance works here to Hawthorne's
purpose. Though nothing in the early part of the novel gives us license
to think that it can possibly be a romance, the shadow of novelistic
convention colors our reading. That, and the combined force of Hester's desire and our acceptance of her as heroine, for it is part of reading a story to desire what our favorite character desires. Clearly,
Hester is very much in love with Dimmesdale, which is to say that she
desires him.

Of course, love stories can have sad endings as well as happy ones,
and the conclusion to "The Prison-Door" has told us that this is a
story with a "darkening close," a "tale of human frailty and sorrow"
(48). But a sad love story can be, for readers, as pleasurable in its own
way as a happy one; and a sad love story is quite a different matter
from no love story at all! Therefore, we continue to expect against the
odds that *The Scarlet Letter* will reveal itself to be a love story. And
so it does, with this twist: that the love story cannot be separated from
the matter of the revelation of Dimmesdale's identity as Hester's lover.

After the first four chapters the novel is plotted as a sequence of reunions between Hester and Dimmesdale, with material between such encounters preparing for them. First, there is a meeting in Governor Bellingham's house, late in the summer some three years after the opening of the action (chapter 8). This is when the magistrates are thinking of taking Pearl away from Hester and she goes to argue with them. Much of this scene, like the chapters that precede it, is devoted to bringing out Hester's character, especially her increasing self-sufficiency and readiness to stand up to authority; and to developing her relation with Pearl as well as the character of the child. In due time Pearl will emerge as a significant complication of the relationship between Hester and Dimmesdale; in an important sense she already is such a complication, for she, who is the incarnation of her parents' affair, has also put an end to it. In that there would be no scarlet letter had there been no Pearl, she is the story's cause, and there can be no meeting between Hester and Dimmesdale without her. If Hester had lost Pearl, she would have reacted violently by turning to witchcraft, thus validating the authorities' view of her. This would have ended her chances of changing the meaning of the letter. She must keep the child to keep her struggle going.

The scene in Bellingham's house also gives us our first exposure to Dimmesdale since the early scaffold scene; he is not to move to the center of the stage until chapter 9. As in the scene at the marketplace, this meeting between Hester and Dimmesdale, taking place under the eye of authority, is characterized by duplicity and concealment on the part of both lovers, although for different reasons. Hester conceals for Dimmesdale's sake, Dimmesdale for his own. In his ministerial role Dimmesdale argues on Hester's behalf. The surface betrays no hint of the true relations between the characters, although the possibility of rupture is apparent to the reader and creates a certain amount of suspense. Chillingworth is there too, another watchful eye from whom truths must be hidden.

The second meeting (chapter 12) takes place at night on the scaffold, in May, nearly four years after the episode at Bellingham's. This meeting, in real time seven years from the beginning of the action, occurs only halfway through the novel. During this encounter, when

Hester and Pearl stand beside Dimmesdale and share his mock penance, Hester realizes the depth of his suffering and the extent of his deterioration. Her realization leads to a decision: she will tell him who Chillingworth is. We have seen, in intervening chapters, both Dimmesdale's decline and Hester's remarkable growth in self-sufficiency, both of which are necessary to the decision that Hester takes in chapter 13, "Another View of Hester." In chapter 13, however, Hawthorne goes further than he did in his earlier consideration of Hester, making a point of the extent to which Hester has become her own law. This is a crucial development since, in the climactic reunion in the forest, Hester will present herself to Dimmesdale as an alternative to Puritan law.

Hester figures her decision in language that has heroic echoes: she "resolved to meet her former husband, and do what might be in her power for the rescue of the victim" (167). The reversal of sex roles, from the point of view of traditional stories, is most interesting: Dimmesdale is like the captive maiden and Hester the knight who will sally out to do battle for him. Naturally, she must first combat Chillingworth, the dragon or wizard (and he is as much a wizard as he is a physician) who guards the prison. He is rather quickly dispatched, in this fairy-tale frame—he really has no power over Hester—and she can now proceed to the heart of her mission, to rescue Dimmesdale from his own despair, from himself.

Hester has moved quickly, and this climactic meeting (chapters 17, 18, 19) takes place in the forest soon after her talk with Chillingworth (which occurred soon after the midnight scaffold scene—the pace of the novel is speeding up). So far as she is in control of her own motives, Hester has intended no more than to tell Dimmesdale who Chillingworth is so that he can take whatever action seems appropriate to extricate himself from the physician's clutches. That is to say, her idea of rescuing Dimmesdale goes no further than to alert him to his danger. But she finds a man so demoralized that she is impelled, by her own strong and active nature as well as by his direct appeal ("Be thou strong for me," "advise me what to do" [196]), to go far beyond her original intention. First she advises him to leave the Puritan settlement, suggesting (as symbolic alternatives) that he go west to the wilderness, or east to the Old World.

Dimmesdale rejects both suggestions: "thou tellest of running a race to a man whose knees are tottering beneath him! I must die here. There is not the strength or courage left me to venture into the wide, strange, difficult world, alone!" And then he repeats the word: "Alone, Hester!" Here is, evidently, an invitation difficult for a woman in love to refuse, and Hester does not refuse it. "Thou shalt not go alone," she answers (198). At this point, with the lovers united, or reunited, *The Scarlet Letter* certainly reveals itself as a love story. And yet, if the lovers run off together, what happens to the other plot lines? Certainly Hester's standing in the community, which has been slowly rising, will plummet again; once and for all she will be typed as a sinful, fallen woman.

And as for Dimmesdale, the plot tending toward his own disclosure of his identity as Hester's lover will be abandoned: the community will be able to deduce it, but he will not have confessed it himself. Which is to say that, as the love story behind *The Scarlet Letter* reveals itself, it also reveals itself as the adversary of the main story that *The Scarlet Letter* is trying to tell, which has to do with the aftermath of committing an act that sets one at odds with one's society. The fact is that running away from society cannot possibly resolve the issues that such a plot has raised.

Apparently the love story requires, for its fulfillment, denying the claims of society altogether. And although it is possible to rebel against society, it is not possible (at least not in the world that *The Scarlet Letter* has created) to deny society's causal and constitutive role in life. Hester and Dimmesdale are where they are, as they are, not only because of what they did but equally—perhaps more—because of how their deed was viewed and marked by society. The idea of a love without context, which glimmers beautifully before Hester and Dimmesdale in the forest, is a delusion. Such a delusion is what conventional love stories give their readers. Their validation of love requires the removal of love from any social milieu. There is no way, at this late point in *The Scarlet Letter,* to extricate Hester and Dimmesdale from their social milieu.

And, in fact, within the context of the society that encloses them, their love idyll cannot be seen as anything else except a repetition of their initial act, whatever we may wish to call it: sin, crime, or something with "a consecration of its own," as Hester says (195). Their joint decision to flee does over again what they originally did, with this difference: that while the first time they were carried away by passion, this time they know perfectly well what they are doing. The first "sin" (or whatever) was unpremeditated; this one is self-aware and deliberate. Seven years, the narrator says, have only tended to this moment, which represents a point of much greater separation from society than either, each alienated in a different way, has reached before. The story has thus arrived at its point of greatest tension.

But, for the moment, the lovers in the forest seem free to act out their idyll without regard for consequences. In accord with that idyll, and in what is surely one of the great moments in American (or any other) literature, Hester removes the scarlet letter from her gown (the moment romantic readers have been waiting for) and the cap from her hair, and reverts at once to the beautiful and happy woman that she had been before. And at just this point, where the liberated love story reaches its height, Pearl returns from the further depths of the forest where she has been playing. Even in the forest, after all, the lovers are not free. And from this point on the plot begins to descend from the apex, and the forest scene takes its place in the story as an event that leads to the opposite of what the lovers (or at least Hester) intended.

When Hester resumes wearing the letter, and puts on her cap again, the lovers (less enlightened than the readers who have been told by the narrator, after all, that this tale has a darkening close) believe that their setback is only temporary. They leave the forest with plans to sail to Europe on the next available ship. The forest scene does not come to a full stop, however, until Dimmesdale has safely returned to his chamber; and on his walk home (chapter 20, "The Minister in a Maze," which nicely balances chapter 13, "Another View of Hester") there is plenty of evidence that freedom for him is not the same thing as it is for Hester. This chapter, which so clearly contrasts the two lovers, helps to guarantee that even the most intense devotees of romantic love will not be desolated at the failure of the lovers' joint project. Much as we tend to want for the protagonist what she wants for herself, we cannot see in Dimmesdale what she sees. Does he love her? We learn in this chapter that the minister was delighted by news that the next available ship will not leave Boston before he has a chance to preach his election sermon. His "priorities," as we might say today, don't accord with an ideal romantic love, and this is not the first suggestion that "love" is not really reciprocal between them. As Dimmesdale decides to go with Hester, he is shown thinking "neither can I any longer live without her companionship; so powerful is she to sustain,—so tender to soothe" (201). Not a thought of doing anything for her; only what is in the relationship for him. Here is a second way in which the love story is doubly a delusion: it is, perhaps, purely Hester's creation, built from her desire on the sands of Dimmesdale's weakness. In refusing to be a love story, *The Scarlet Letter* may be a critique of the idea of romantic love.

Approaching the conclusion of *The Scarlet Letter,* let us stop to schematize the plot thus far. There is a beginning of four chapters; a middle of sixteen chapters, punctuated by a key scene in chapter 12—the midpoint of the book and of the middle section as well. Four chapters remain. The introductory section is concluded by an action—Hester's oath (chapter 4)—which leads to the middle section of the book when the main characters are united in a plot concerning the rescue of Dimmesdale from his intolerable hypocrisy, via the revelation of his identity as Hester's lover. In structural terms, Hester is the protagonist of this story, Chillingworth the antagonist, and Dimmesdale the desirable object that both are struggling to possess. How, we might ask, does Hester's desire to protect Dimmesdale represent a desire to possess him? The one seems so altruistic, the other so selfish. But, of course, protection is a form of possession and, as we shall see, Dimmesdale's ultimate confession does indeed mean that Hester loses him. Remember, though, that this plot is framed within the larger narrative of Hester's struggle with the Puritan community. In that narrative, her desire to possess Dimmesdale represents a delusion from which she needs to be separated.

After sharing Dimmesdale's night vigil on the scaffold (chapter 12), Hester realizes that Chillingworth has discovered Dimmesdale's identity and is using his knowledge to cause harm. She thereupon decides to break her oath, precipitating the climax of the book (chapters 17–19), which, in turn, leads to the finale. She meets with Dimmesdale in the forest and tells him who Chillingworth is; the upshot of this meeting is a joint decision to leave Boston and go back together to Europe. This forest scene occurs in the second half of the middle, or about two-thirds along. Thus, as well as dividing the story into carefully proportioned beginning (one sixth), middle (two-thirds), and end (one sixth), we can divide the story into thirds, in half, and into segments of four chapters each. Manifestly, *The Scarlet Letter* has been carefully constructed with an eye to symmetry and proportion, that is, with an old-fashioned sense of beauty and order. Sad, but beautiful: like the letter that gives it its name—and not coincidentally.

In the three chapters that come after "The Minister in a Maze" we return to the marketplace where the action began. This is another indication of symmetry: in fact, the opening, middle, and closing scenes of the action are all set in the marketplace and center on the scaffold. Chapter 12, however, is a sort of dark mirror of the first and last scaffold scenes, since it takes place at night, with the marketplace deserted, whereas the other two occur in daylight, on occasions of public significance. Hawthorne stresses the fatality of his design in chapter 22, when he has Hester stop at the foot of the pillory and remain, kept there by "an irresistible feeling" (242). And as she stops there, a crowd assembles around her to stare at the scarlet letter, exactly as they had done seven years before. "Hester saw and recognized the self-same faces of that group of matrons, who had awaited her forthcoming from the prison-door, seven years ago"; again she stands "in that magic circle of ignominy, where the cunning cruelty of her sentence seemed to have fixed her for ever" (246). Once more, as on that other occasion, Hester is in a low place and Dimmesdale in a high one, once again he is preaching to an infatuated multitude. The whole story seems to have circled round, to have returned hopelessly to its beginnings at the very moment of escape.

But escape is already undermined, for Chillingworth has learned their plans and intends to go along. To go through the world together with Chillingworth would obviously be no escape at all. At this last moment, then, it is Hester who needs rescue, as much from Dimmesdale as from her scarlet letter. For Dimmesdale, her great love, is also her great illusion; he is not the man she imagined, or he is (in her mind) an imaginary man. Yet it is for his sake that she has worn the letter all these years. It is a wonderful twist to the plot, then, that the real Dimmesdale rescues her from her infatuation. He is, in fact, a dying man; the great sermon he just preached has drained almost all the life remaining in him. He has just enough energy for one more act—his long-delayed confession. It is an act performed to save his own soul, and he calls upon Hester's physical and moral strength to aid him in carrying it out. But, whatever his motives, it frees Hester, as well as Pearl.

Dimmesdale's death on the scaffold is not the end of the novel. For all the interest his character and dilemma may hold (and presumably all the important characters in a novel should be interesting), he is not the main character in this fiction. In a chapter simply titled "Conclusion" Hawthorne covers a space of many years, during which time Chillingworth dies and leaves all his money to Pearl; Hester and Pearl depart for Europe; and, finally, Hester returns alone to Boston, resumes life in her isolated cottage, and continues to wear the scarlet letter even though "not the sternest magistrate of that iron period would have imposed it." Now, "the scarlet letter ceased to be a stigma which attracted the world's scorn and bitterness, and became a type of something to be sorrowed over, and looked upon with awe, yet with reverence too" (263). This is not quite what Hester had in mind in her earlier years, when she had embroidered the letter with fantastic flourishes of gold thread; it cannot be said that she triumphs, on her own terms, over the community. But perhaps her own terms have changed. And certainly, she has traveled far from the position of scorn and ignominy that she occupied in the opening scene. Is this a happy ending? Not in the same sense that Pearl's story has a happy ending, for apparently she has made an aristocratic marriage somewhere in Europe. Not, perhaps, in any sense that a romantic reader can comfortably accept. But Hester has certainly changed the Puritans more than they have changed her, and more than anybody might have dared to hope at the beginning, when all were so firmly set against her.

2

WHERE?
THE SETTING

Every fiction must locate its action and characters in a world that fits them; we will no more accept Gothic characters in a realistic novel than we will accept realistic characters in a Gothic tale. In *The Scarlet Letter* Hawthorne creates a world that exists—as he himself characterizes it in "The Custom-House" essay—as "a neutral territory, somewhere between the real world and fairy-land, where the Actual and the Imaginary may meet, and each imbue itself with the nature of the other" (36). In such a world characters who are only partly imitative of real life, behaving in ways somewhat removed from the ordinary, seem natural. The important point is that while *The Scarlet Letter* is not "realistic," as we understand the term—and was not intended to be—neither is it a pure fantasy.

THE HISTORICAL SETTING

Within the first few paragraphs of the work Hawthorne seems to establish the action quite specifically in place and time. We are in colonial Boston, among the first generation of Puritan settlers, those who emigrated from the Old World to the New (as opposed to those who would later be born there). The topography is precise: the first prison is "in the vicinity of Cornhill," the cemetery "on Isaac Johnson's lot, and round about his grave," a spot that subsequently, the narrator goes on to say, was to become "the nucleus of all the congregated sepulchres in the old church-yard of King's Chapel" (47). Not only does Hawthorne seem to know what he is talking about; scholarly research has shown that he did know, and that in all probability he had Caleb H. Snow's reliable work of 1825, *A History of Boston, the Metropolis of Massachusetts,* on his table for reference as he wrote *The Scarlet Letter.*

He had read widely in New England history during his sojourn in Salem between 1825 and 1837, but it is impossible to say how much of that reading, carried out so long before the writing of *The Scarlet Letter,* he remembered. Apparently he did not take notes when he read, so we can only tell what aspects of the record impressed him by seeing what he did with it in his fiction. Comparison of details indicates that in composing *The Scarlet Letter* he used (along with Snow's book) Joseph B. Felt's *The Annals of Salem, from Its First Settlement* (1827); editions of Cotton Mather's *Magnalia Christi Americana* (1702) and *Wonders of the Invisible World* (1693); and probably an 1825 edition of John Winthrop's *History of New England,* edited by James Savage (the only text that identifies Mistress Hibbins as Governor Bellingham's sister).

Every working writer quickly learns that a text must contain specific details if it is to make any impression on a reader at all; and from his opening reference to the "gray, steeple-crowned hats" worn by Puritan men (47) to his description of Puritan holiday pastimes—"wrestling-matches, in the differing fashions of Cornwall and Devonshire," "a friendly bout at quarterstaff," "an exhibition with the buckler and broadsword" (231)—Hawthorne is doing what a good writer has to do. And upon investigation, we find that the details that he has scattered through *The Scarlet Letter* are not only striking and picturesque, but basically accurate.

Yet, when we try to place the story exactly in time, the accuracy becomes illusory, precision vanishes. Hawthorne begins by saying that it is "some fifteen or twenty years after the settlement of the town"

(47)—a careful gesture, one might say, in the direction of uncertainty, since five years of history can make a tremendous difference. Thereafter he makes several mistakes that are most curious for one who was working closely with historical references. One datable historical event within the confines of the action, for example, is the death of Governor Winthrop. This takes place on the night of the minister's vigil, when, standing on the scaffold, he sees a great *A* in the sky. Snow and other sources say that Winthrop died on 26 March 1649. But Hawthorne, who omits the year, carefully places it on a Saturday night (the next day is the Sabbath [157]) in "early May" (147). While offering reasons for the change in the month, scholars seeking for certainty have chosen to assume that the year should be taken as a fixed point in the narrative, although one might logically argue that one deviation from the record undercuts all other certainties.

But taking June 1649 for the third scaffold scene—as we must since it occurs about a month after Winthrop's death— creates chronological problems. Hawthorne repeats several times that seven years have elapsed between the opening of the story and its culmination; therefore we must date the first scaffold scene in June 1642. This is what many scholars have assumed, but it will not work. First, Bellingham, governor of the colony in 1641, was defeated by John Winthrop in the election of May 1642; thus he would no longer have been governor at the story's opening. (He was again elected governor in 1654, and from 1665 to 1672, but neither of these dates fits the chronology either.) Second, Anne Hutchinson had been expelled from the colony in 1638, a mere four years previously, and was not to die until 1643. The reference to her as "sainted" would thus seem premature, unless the term has a specific and highly ironic theological reference, taking Hutchinson as one of the Puritan elect. Most crucially, since the Massachusetts Bay Colony was settled in 1630, and since we begin "some fifteen or twenty years after the settlement," 1642 is simply too early; crude arithmetic shows that the action must start between 1645 and 1650, with the third scaffold scene taking place between 1652 and 1657. Thus, though Hawthorne has given us a five-year leeway for the initial action, it is a leeway that definitely excludes the one specific event that we can fix chronologically, the death of Governor Winthrop.

There are different ways of thinking about this fuzzy chronology. Most obvious is to say that although Hawthorne got much of his history right, he also got some of it wrong. With so much correct detail, he succeeds in evoking the sense of the times, and we do not need from a novelist what we would rightly demand of a historian. And indeed, since even historians make mistakes, it seems to be asking too much of any human being that his work be error-free.

Another approach is to say that, even though Hawthorne was liable to error like the rest of us, nevertheless, since he was working with historical sources, each deviation may have a purpose behind it; and we can then attempt to fathom the purpose in every case. Attempts have been made by Hawthorne scholars, and they have taken two directions. First, critics suggest that Hawthorne departed from the historical record for technical reasons—to keep his plot smooth and the narration economical. Bellingham, for instance, did live at one margin of the marketplace, so that in his midnight vigil Dimmesdale really could have seen him looking out the window; to bring several governors into the story and develop each character might dissipate its intense effect; therefore, among several possible governors, Hawthorne chose this one. Similarly, if he wanted to end the minister's story at the scaffold in June, thus echoing the initial June scaffold scene, and if he also wanted to speed up the pacing toward the end, he would do better to put the midnight vigil later in the year than the month of March, when Winthrop actually died. In any case, given the New England climate, even an anguished minister might have thought twice about spending most of the night outdoors.

Other scholars, however, quite reasonably point out that Hawthorne might as well have put the right governor in the wrong place, as the wrong governor in the right place, and that a rationale for his deviations should be sought in a historical rather than a formal intention. For example, there is no authority for having Mistress Hibbins reside in her brother's house (assuming that Bellingham was her brother, as only one source does); she had a dwelling of her own, as well as a husband, until 1654. She was imprisoned in 1655, executed as a witch in 1656. A formalist critic might say that Hawthorne placed her as he did for the sake of economy, while the "historicist" critic would counter that he did it to connect Puritan law and Puritan crime—to show that these were two sides of the same coin, inseparable from each other. For the formal critic, the historical world is used by Hawthorne in the service of his fictional intentions. The historicist reverses these priorities and claims that Hawthorne uses his fiction in the service of his historical intentions, which are to provide a searching commentary on the early Puritans.

There is a third way of interpreting Hawthorne's use of history in *The Scarlet Letter,* and this encompasses both approaches above, even though they might seem incompatible with each other. This is to assume that Hawthorne meant specifically to evoke the world of the first-generation Puritans, but also meant to avoid any precision greater than that. As we all know, historical division into generations is useful but necessarily imprecise at best since people are continuously being born and growing old. We may suggest, therefore, that Hawthorne's deviations from the record are designed, not to produce specific historical insights, but rather to generalize his history into an account of an entire generation's experience. Since there is no such thing, really, as "the" experience of "one" generation, Hawthorne has produced a composite, and as part of that composite he has carefully made it impossible for us to come up with a sound chronology for the events of *The Scarlet Letter.* They take place sometime between 1640 and 1660; we can get no more precise than that.

But having accepted some degree of historical purpose in *The Scarlet Letter,* we must notice that Hawthorne's representation of key tenets of Puritan theology is wrong. Here I refer not to the after-the-fact judgments and analysis of the narrator, which are clearly of the nineteenth century, but rather to the religious beliefs and practices of the seventeenth-century characters themselves. In the first place, the characters seldom speak of God, and of the twenty-one occurrences of the word in *The Scarlet Letter,* close to half of them are used in rather unorthodox—from a Puritan perspective—circumstances, as when

Hester argues that she has a right to Pearl because God gave the child to her. The word *Providence,* which we find fourteen times, is used by characters and narrator alike more often in a secularized nineteenth-century sense of "fate" or "destiny" than in the Puritan sense of a specific divine intention or intervention.

There are no references to any particular personage of the Trinity, whereas the idea of the Trinity and the separateness, yet oneness, of its members was basic to Puritan thinking. There are no biblical references, whereas the Puritans constantly quoted Scripture. There are no references to grace, a concept that obsessed them; only two references to salvation and one to redemption; only one to "the infernal pit" (in the sermon that Wilson preaches on the day of Hester's humiliation [68]). The concept of the chosen, or elect, who were also called "saints" by the Puritans, a concept closely tied to the idea of grace, figures only once (in Reverend Wilson's imagined dream about the "glorified saints" [150–51]; and the only election referred to is of the political variety. The ritual of testifying publicly to a conversion experience before admission to church membership is also mentioned once only, when Dimmesdale, returning from the forest, encounters a maiden "newly won" to the faith (219).

Dimmesdale's public confession, which claims certain salvation for him, is—from the Puritan point of view—simple heresy. For Puritan theology was rooted in two related doctrines. First, original sin: Adam's disobedience to God's command (related in the opening chapters of the Book of Genesis in the Old Testament) had marked all his descendants as sinners. The idea was not that people were all weak and capable of sinning: it was, more austerely, that all people had in fact sinned—they were born sinners. Second, predestination: God had picked out certain people to save, and had done so from the beginning of time. Therefore, nothing a person might do could affect his or her candidacy for salvation. It was all already ordained. Christ, to the Puritans, had come to earth to redeem only those who were "elected" or "predestinated." Behind these doctrines lay the tremendous awe and respect that the Puritans felt for divinity, which they expressed by stressing the enormous gap between God and humankind. To imagine that you could be "good enough" to "deserve" salvation was an affront to divine majesty. To imagine that you understood God's purposes well enough to know who should, and who should not, be saved, was also presumptuous. In fact, Anne Hutchinson was particularly condemned for claiming that she had been enlightened as to who in the colony had been elected. For the original American Puritans, these difficult doctrines were the heart of religious belief.

Evidently, neither of these doctrines functions in *The Scarlet Letter;* indeed, on occasion they appear to be specifically denied. "Wouldst thou avenge thyself on the innocent babe?" Hester asks Chillingworth (72)—a nice nineteenth-century sentiment, later repeated by the supposedly orthodox Dimmesdale and accepted by Wilson and Bellingham when they consider taking Pearl away from her mother. The doctrine of original sin established that no human being, even an infant, was an innocent. Again, both Hester and Dimmesdale appear to believe seriously what no true Puritan could have believed, that no other human beings than they have sinned in the world (87)—and the narrator praises them for it. A Puritan might think himself the worst sinner in the world, but obviously the doctrine of original sin made it impossible for one to maintain that only the self was sinful. Hawthorne's Puritans, thus, neither talk nor think like their seventeenth-century "models"; Hawthorne has simply cut out the heart of their theology, making them much more like liberal Christians of the nineteenth century. In this more liberal context the obsession with sin and evil, with sinfulness and sinners, floats about detached from the theological context in which it had its historical place, and becomes an inexplicable outcropping of the Puritan group psyche. Perhaps Hawthorne meant simply to say that "the Puritans were like that." Or, perhaps, by detaching the concept of sin from its theological basis he meant to emphasize the way in which the concept was used by the Puritan rulers for political rather than religious reasons.

Thus, while we may certainly grant that some kind of historical commentary is part of Hawthorne's purpose in *The Scarlet Letter,* we have to realize that historical commentary is not equivalent to historical *accuracy*—indeed, historical commentary often *requires* historical distortion in order to make its points strongly. And we have to remember that Hawthorne never presented himself to the world as a historian, but always as a storyteller or romancer, who intended to create fictional worlds that both were and were not true to actuality. Even if some of the historicist explanations are stimulating and intriguing, we cannot dismiss the probability that when he made intentional changes in the record Hawthorne did so for the purpose of telling his story in a better way. His setting evokes the historical record without being committed to it, providing the atmosphere for characters who both are and are not beings in history.

THE MARVELOUS AND THE SYMBOLIC

Besides "actuality," the other contributor to the "neutral territory" of Hawthorne's special kind of fiction is what he called the "imaginary," and one reason for his setting his work back in time is this: since the historical world obviously no longer exists, we can quite easily see that a powerful act of imagination is required to bring it back to us. For many historical novelists of Hawthorne's time (and ours) historical fiction aims to disguise the necessary role of imagination, creating a world that, by the denseness of its detail and the accuracy of its particulars, would conceal the agency of the imagination that has made it. The reader would be fooled into thinking that the novelist had simply imitated what was before him; the imagination would become, so to speak, transparent. Hawthorne felt that such an illusion of reality, no matter how pleasurable it might be, was completely false; and not only for historical fiction. All represented reality had to be the product in part of the particular imagination that represented it. At the same time that he wanted readers to accept his world as real, he wanted them to do so without forgetting that it was fictional, because he believed that the pleasure of fiction was heightened when we recall that it is something like magic. We wouldn't appreciate a magician's tricks if we forgot that they were magic, after all. Beyond this, at some level Hawthorne thought that there was no such thing as an objective reality; there were only different realities as composed through the focusing and selecting lenses of different perceivers, and none of the lenses was absolutely transparent or distortion-free. He felt that he could better represent this view if he created a fictional world that contained a significant admixture of the imaginary, rather than simply writing one more realistic fiction with its focus on ordinary details in the everyday, contemporary world. Although he respected the achievements of the new literary realism, he was imaginatively fatigued by the lengthy chronicling of the humdrum that realism required from the writer.

And the early Puritan world suited him for more reasons than its chronological remoteness. One of these other reasons is that it could be presented as a relatively "empty" and simple time. Unlike the Old World of seventeenth-century Europe, the Massachusetts Bay Colony was thinly populated, surrounded by great tracts of virtually uninhabited space, had a very simple and largely uniform style of life among all its people, lacked large cities and the complex cultural and conventional behavior they imply, and was cut off by the Atlantic Ocean and a long, perilous sea journey from its origins.

That Hawthorne found these qualities of early New England congenial to his aims is evidenced by the fact that he markedly exaggerated them in *The Scarlet Letter.* The sailors, the Indians, the Quakers, Reverend Blackstone, the indentured servant at Governor Bellingham's—here and there an allusion reaches out to the more complex and cosmopolitan cultural web in which the first generation of Puritans was enmeshed, but the economic, domestic, and intellectual life of the colony is largely missing, and, on the whole, Boston comes to us as though it were a settlement on an otherwise unpopulated planet. In fact, despite the difficulty and length of the journey, the early Massachusetts Puritans sailed to and from Old England constantly; letters and goods came and went on every ship. At the same time, other settlements—Rhode Island, New Amsterdam, Virginia, breakaway Puritan colonies in Massachusetts and Connecticut—increasingly filled the eastern states. During the years in which the events of *The Scarlet Letter* unfold, England was embroiled in a Civil War; on 30 January

1649 King Charles was beheaded and a Puritan government took over the country. These events were, obviously, of the first importance to a Puritan colony; the "real" Boston would have been buzzing with them, most especially in the spring and summer of that year when, according to some scholars, the final scaffold scene takes place. But there is nothing of this in *The Scarlet Letter*.

A second appeal of the early Puritan world to Hawthorne was that its inhabitants were pre-scientific, pre-empirical, pre-rational. By leaving Europe when they did, the Puritans "missed," so to speak, many of the great philosophical developments of the seventeenth century. Francis Bacon (1561–1616) elaborated a method for doing experiments in which hypotheses were tested and conclusions derived from repeated observation; Thomas Hobbes (1588–1679) suggested that society was the human creation of beings who had banded together for self-protection; René Descartes (1596–1650) offered a view of mind separated from nature and therefore able to observe it without bias; John Locke (1632–1704) suggested that ideas in the mind originated entirely in sensory perceptions. In Europe, as Hawthorne says in *The Scarlet Letter*, "it was an age in which the human intellect, newly emancipated, had taken a more active and a wider range than for many centuries before" (164); but not so in the New World, where Hester, had her radical thoughts been known to the authorities, would probably have been put to death.

Thus, the Puritans, however they might have imagined themselves in the forefront of their age, in many respects remained profoundly medieval in their worldview. And their mode of thinking was also characterized by some very specific procedures, above all the habit of "interpreting" everything that they saw, everything that happened to them, as a message from God with specific import for them. They had no doubt that their mission into the New World was directly demanded by God, and that He was constantly overseeing their work and letting them know whether He was pleased or displeased with it. So the Puritans did not live in the "real world" either, as we might understand that concept today; they lived in a world that was both a challenge set out for them by God and a text that recorded his message, but that never existed in and for itself. To dismiss an interpretation as "fantasy" and to call the tangible object that called forth the interpretation the "reality" would have seemed to them grotesque.

The Puritans, rather than believing that witchcraft was a fantasy, had developed complex procedures for determining whether the specter that manifested itself came from God or, deceptively, from the Devil. The reality of the specter, however, was not to be doubted. The Puritans had thus no procedures that we would recognize for distinguishing between their fantasies and reality, or between the natural and the supernatural; and in a sense their "real" world was "really" imaginary. And, of course, in such a world, many people seriously practiced witchcraft and believed themselves to be witches. So, to the extent that Hawthorne wanted to create a fiction in which actual and imaginary did more than meet—a fiction in which each took part of its nature from the other—his task was made easier by the choice of the early Puritan setting.

Then, too, he was himself a New Englander descended from these Puritans, a fact that would make their worldview and mind-set matters of personal interest, especially insofar as he recognized a tendency in his own imagination that might seem to resemble theirs. The setting of *The Scarlet Letter*, therefore, cannot be adequately described by referring to its location in historical time and space, and carefully pointing out or providing explanations for Hawthorne's departures from historical record. As every reader recognizes, this is a setting in which the supernatural and symbolic have been given real existence and real efficacy, as would have been the case for colonial Puritans of the seventeenth century; and in this sense the setting is more "true" to the Puritan mind than a work guided by modern principles of historical accuracy.

There are many obvious cases in *The Scarlet Letter* where the supernatural or, as Hawthorne preferred to call it, the marvelous, is real, and all the more so because Hawthorne generally accompanies such instances with alternative explanations, by appearing to dismiss—but not really doing so—the marvelous as product of superstitious fancy, or by offering a naturalistic cause for the event. Take, for instance, the marvelous powers of Hester's scarlet letter, perhaps the most striking supernatural object. Those who have read "The Custom-House" already know that the letter has marvelous powers. Others meet it first as a curious piece of wonderful embroidery with terrible import for the wearer: an unusual, but not a supernatural object. We first read of the letter's supernatural radiance in terms that allow us to dismiss the marvelous as an increment to the letter created by Puritan superstition: "it was whispered, by those who peered after her, that the scarlet letter threw a lurid gleam along the dark passage-way of the interior" (69). Later, when the narrator says straightforwardly that "there glimmered the embroidered letter, with comfort in its unearthly ray" (161), we are perhaps free to dismiss the word *unearthly* as narratorial enthusiasm and think that the letter glows with nothing more than the light reflected from the gold threads of its embroidery. We are free to do so, but we don't.

The letter also has the capacity to inflict physical pain on Hester, to burn her; and it does so with special intensity when she is in the company of secret sin. The pain may be no more than the constant aching of her heart, the throb no more than the heightened sensitivity that her suffering has created: "It now and then appeared to Hester,—if altogether fancy, it was nevertheless too potent to be resisted,—she felt or fancied, then, that the scarlet letter had endowed her with a new sense. She shuddered to believe, yet could not help believing, that it gave her a sympathetic knowledge of the hidden sin in other hearts" (86). The narrator protects himself, yet we finally will not reason away every appearance of the marvelous, because there are too many of them. Why not accept the shorthand, so to speak, of the text: Hester has indeed been given a particular power of insight through the agency of the letter.

Another major instance of the marvelous in *The Scarlet Letter* is the physical deterioration of Chillingworth as he pursues his revenge. This physical deterioration is conveyed to us through Hester's observations in chapter 14, and so could be attributed to her seventeenth-century imagination; but it is reinforced by the narrator's account. "Ever and anon, too, there came a glare of red light out of his eyes; as if the old man's soul were on fire, and kept on smouldering duskily within his breast" (169). In Chillingworth, the narrator goes on, can be seen "a striking evidence of man's faculty of transforming himself into a devil" (170). Then, a little further on, we read that he let "the lurid fire of his heart blaze out before her eyes" (171); perhaps a metaphor only, and yet the meshing of levels of description here makes it quite impossible for us to believe that there is not, somehow, a "real" fire in Chillingworth's heart.

A third is the way in which Pearl, quite deliberately dressed by her mother to resemble the scarlet letter, closely corresponds to it. We can explain her fascination with the letter and her lawless behavior as aspects of the intense relationship she has with Hester; but we cannot explain it altogether in this way. Like Chillingworth, Pearl is a character with partial status as allegory, and in order to make her "work" as both a real child and an allegorical presence, Hawthorne envelops her in an ambience of the unlikely: do her feet touch the ground? do the animals of the forest sympathize with her? is there, from time to time, a fiend peeping out of her eyes? Almost certainly, yes.

Of course, the treatment of witches, in the person of Mistress Hibbins, allows for the marvelous. The story is rich in details of witchcraft (most of which Hawthorne drew from a source much later than the time period with which he is dealing, the writings of Cotton Mather). There is no doubt that Mistress Hibbins is a real, a practicing witch; and we are not invited to think of her as one who is deluded by her own superstitions, or by psychopathology. She knows what she is talking about; her perceptions are certain, her ground is firm.

Although Hester's *A* is probably the chief instance of the marvelous, the second half of the plot turns with almost equal significance on a second and equally though differently remarkable *A*; the one that is inscribed on Dimmesdale's chest and revealed to the people at the third scaffold scene. How is this *A* to be explained? Some critics have followed the naturalistic hint and studied nineteenth-century herbals and medical texts to discover diseases or drugs that Hawthorne might have known that would be capable of producing such an eruption. But in running through his catalog of alternatives, Hawthorne quite clearly aligns himself with the supernatural explanation; here, for once, the multitude is anxious to explain the letter in any way but the "real" one.

> Some affirmed that the Reverend Mr. Dimmesdale . . . had begun a course of penance . . . by inflicting a hideous torture on himself. Others contended that . . . old Roger Chillingworth . . . had caused it to appear, through the agency of magic and poisonous drugs. Others, again—*and those best able to appreciate the minister's peculiar sensibility, and the wonderful operation of his spirit upon the body,*—whispered their belief, that the awful symbol was the effect of the ever-active tooth of remorse. (258, emphasis added)

Of course, Hawthorne's use of the supernatural does not mean that he believed in it. He did intend to imply, almost certainly, that explanations that split mind or spirit from matter and insisted on purely material or mechanical causes had only limited usefulness; we might call his view "holistic" today. In addition, as a storyteller and entertainer, he used the marvelous as any good narrator does: to heighten his effects, to intensify his contrasts, to provide some extra shivers (and hence enjoyment) for his audience. The demand that every fiction be tested by the criterion of verisimilitude seemed to him a tremendous narrowing of imaginative scope—was imagination not a creative as well as an imitative power?

Our account of the setting of *The Scarlet Letter* is still not adequate, even when we have added acknowledgment of the presence of the marvelous to our location of the story in a corrected historical time and space. For part of our experience of the setting is its symbolic quality. It is a world whose inhabitants utilize allegorical and symbolic modes of thinking, and who attribute real efficacy to the symbols they have established. But this, after all, allowing for different symbols in different cultures, would still be a world like our own. The world of *The Scarlet Letter* is also the product of such symbolizing on the part of the storyteller. The symbol of the scarlet letter is only one—albeit the most striking and focused—of many. No more than any Puritan can we take the forest simply as a forest, Indians as those who happened to be earlier settlers, the ocean as a massive body of water. The setting of *The Scarlet Letter* is in part a series of symbolic contrasts around a constellation of repeated images.

Probably the two most important contrasts are those of light and dark, and of town and forest (clearing and wilderness). The polarity of light and dark shows up in the constant interplay of sunshine and shadow during the day, and of daytime and nighttime in the natural cycle. (But light is symbolically divided into sunlight, which comes from heaven, and firelight, which seems to come from the pit. And firelight, again, divides into hellfire and hearthfire. Thus, symbolic worlds are not necessarily easy to read.) In principle, sunlight and daytime are or should be the equivalent of openness, honesty, and goodness; nighttime and shadow represent concealment, secrets, and evil. Similarly, in principle, the settlement represents human connection, community, civilization, while the forest represents isolation, solitude, and savagery. The forest is the abode of the untamed, uncivilized Indian, whom Hester begins to resemble after years of solitude ("her intellect and heart had their home, as it were, in desert places, where she roamed as freely as the wild Indian in his woods" [199]). It is also the home of "the Black Man," the Devil (184–85). The settlement, almost always portrayed in the sunlight, is the home of law, order, civilization, and social behavior. Is it also the home of virtue?

Thus, the two symbolic systems do not simplify; they add rich ambiguity. Wildness and evil are not necessarily identical; the forest, where Indians and the Devil dwell, is also the abode of nature, which the community must destroy in order to erect its civilization. Is nature evil, or only untamed? Is everything that is untamed evil? Why does every heart have secrets, and if every heart does, might not the forest, where they can be shown, be more the abode of honesty than the town, where law and order require inhibition, suppression, and concealment? In town, Dimmesdale can mount the scaffold and enact a mock penance only in darkest night. He can freely be himself with Hester only in the forest, and in the heart of the forest's darkness the

sun bursts out as though to support the lovers' liberty. But he tells
Pearl that he will not take her hand at noontime, in broad daylight, in
the marketplace, and Hester scolds the child for talking about the forest in the marketplace. At length, we sense that the forest is the symbol
for the human heart, and the inner self; thus, if the settlement stands
for the society, it would appear to be a society that has neglected or
even outlawed the human heart. What kind of community can be
erected on a denial of the heart? On the other hand, if the human heart
is evil, what kind of community can be erected that does *not* deny it—
or at least, that does not supervise and police it?

Our real world, of course, does not automatically pose such questions; but Hawthorne's imaginary world does, because he has constructed it to symbolize them. But beyond and beneath the particular
meanings that his symbols bear, and our understanding of the themes
of *The Scarlet Letter* that are implied by them, is the fact that the
setting of the novel is a world built out of symbolic contrasts. There
are images of labyrinths, mazes, and caves; of buried treasures and
buried corpses; of houses and gardens; of flowers and weeds; of gold
and iron; of scarlet and black; of mirrors and reflections. Scarcely a
paragraph in the book fails to develop an image. Thus, when we talk
about symbols and brood about their meanings, we are not performing an obscure act of literary criticism, but responding as we should
and must to the scene that Hawthorne has set in this novel, a scene in
which almost everything is or can become a metaphor or symbol.

Then we can come around to the question of the historical setting
in another way. Having once committed a certain deed, Hester and
Dimmesdale (and Pearl, too, for that matter) are marked by it forever.
They cannot escape it. The Puritan settlement is an event in history
that has, we might imagine, marked the American nation forever, just
as an event in Hester's history marked *her*. Yet, nothing is more attractive to Americans than to imagine that individuals are free of history, able to define themselves, to make themselves in the image of
their desired selves. History then—the Puritans themselves—may be a
symbol in *The Scarlet Letter*, a symbol that requires us to consider the
possibility that a certain past having taken place, we are all its descen-

dants and its victims. The Puritans, that is to say, may be the national *A*.

THE NARRATOR

We have seen that the narrator is an inescapable presence in *The Scarlet Letter* from the very first. He is not a character in the story, in the normal sense of that term, but he is very much a part of the action because the action is constantly subjected to his commentary, interpretation, and criticism.

In fact, it is often extremely difficult, if not impossible, neatly to separate out the narrator's commentary from his presentation and description of things "in themselves" in this novel. For a simple example, consider the report on Dimmesdale's thoughts as he stands on the scaffold during his midnight vigil. As he sees Reverend Wilson approaching, he beholds "his brother clergyman,—or, to speak more accurately, his professional father, as well as highly valued friend" (150). Who is correcting his words here, in order "to speak more accurately"? It can only be the narrator; and since the narrator might have spoken more accurately in the first place (by deleting his less accurate words), his interpolation serves forcefully to remind us of his presence in the scene. Then, when Dimmesdale imagines how the people would respond if they were to find him there in the morning, the text states that "a dusky tumult would flap its wings from one house to another" (151). This poetic image could not be Dimmesdale's thought.

And when the *A* in the sky lights up the little town, the narrator withdraws from Dimmesdale's mind entirely, noting that one could see "the wooden houses, with their jutting stories and quaint gable-peaks . . . visible, but with a singularity of aspect that seemed to give another moral interpretation to the things of this world than they had ever borne before" (154). Not only is the comment about moral interpretation added to the scene by the narrator, as we can easily see; the adjective *quaint* must also emanate from his point of view, since no

Puritans of the time would see their own roof peaks as "quaint." This word establishes that the narrator is removed in time from the action, and it also suggests a point of view that we, as readers, would have of the action if we were present at it. The word is less an objective description of the scene than a description that has taken into account the perspective of the readers. Thus, the narrator serves both as commentator on, and as reader surrogate in, the story. And here is another way in which Hawthorne shows that "reality" is constructed out of points of view, rather than existing independently of perceivers.

Not all novels are told in this manner, even though all novels must be "told." Sometimes novels are told from the perspective of a character within the world of the action, whether the main character or a minor one. Such characters are given appearances, histories, and roles to play. Sometimes novels are told through the perspective of one or more characters within the action, but with these perspectives filtered through a separate and disembodied narrative voice. Often, and commonly in the nineteenth century, novels are told more or less as *The Scarlet Letter* is, by a narrator who is outside and above the world of the action while taking a very active role in transmitting it. In such cases, it is natural to think of that narrator as a fictional representation of the author himself. Thus, sometimes we say "the narrator" and sometimes we say "Hawthorne."

There is nothing wrong in using these terms interchangeably in talking about *The Scarlet Letter* so long as we realize that, as we have seen, the narrator is *not* Hawthorne, in that he does not exist outside the confines of this one book. This narrator is, finally, a basic element in the atmosphere of the novel, an aspect of its setting. Whereas Hawthorne was a person sitting at his desk writing the novel, with such motives in mind as paying his bills and becoming famous, the narrator has no other motive than to narrate. The views he expresses, the analysis he provides, may or may not correspond with what Hawthorne the human being really thought. Thus, even when we use the term *Hawthorne* for this narrator it is important to realize that we do so mainly because we want to give the narrator a name, and that is the only possible name we can give him. But as soon as we give a name to the narrator, we begin to treat him as though he were a *person*, and that may be a mistake.

We may want to identify the narrator with the biographical author because we value sincerity. We think a serious author should write from the heart, and we tend to take the voice of the narrator as articulating the beliefs of the author. Also, we want to find a secure ground for a "correct" interpretation of the story; we want the story to have "authority," and we look for such authority in a narrator, especially when the narrator is free with analysis and commentary. Some critics of *The Scarlet Letter*—especially those who have concerned themselves with its historical accuracy or lack of accuracy—have suggested that the narrator, far from being Hawthorne's deputy, is quite unreliable, and is therefore a kind of ironic figure who cannot be taken as securing the novel's truth. Such an ironic function, however improbable it may appear, cannot entirely be discounted. But it requires us to separate out the narrator from the text as a person—just the thing that we should not do.

Certainly the narrator, when offering specific views, may express an opinion that a particular reader finds hard to accept. In such cases a reader may wish to discover a different meaning in the story from the one the narrator seems trying to give it. When the narrator says that the letter has not done its office for Hester, or that in her solitude she learned much "amiss," those who are attracted to her independence may wish to discount his judgment. Then, in many instances the narrator does not provide a meaning or interpretation where readers might want one. For instance, he is silent about whether Dimmesdale's final confession is sincere, neither commenting on it in his own voice, nor telling us what is in Dimmesdale's mind at that time. Even if the narrator always tells the truth, so to speak, he does not tell us the whole truth. Many questions in *The Scarlet Letter* remain unanswered.

Thus, one attribute of this particular narrator, if you take him as a "person" rather than a "presence," is a frequent willingness to leave explanations open and a concomitant refusal to serve as an authority, a refusal to play the very role that a reader expects from narrators. He pretends that the story exists independently of him and that he does not know its meaning any better than we do. The technique of multiple explanations along with other strategies to create ambiguity enhances our impression of his uncertainty. Since one of the things that *The Scarlet Letter* questions is authority itself, perhaps Hawthorne hesitates to establish an authority within the novel that must be accepted without question.

At the same time that the narrator adopts an attitude of only partial authority over his narrative, he firmly places himself in the nineteenth century. From the very start of the narrative he is constantly reminding his readers of the differences between the Puritan age and the present. There is absolutely no pretense that we are in Puritan times; in fact, there are continual references to the century in which the narrator and the readers live. The action of the novel may take place in Puritan times, but the act of narrating the story and of analyzing and assessing it definitely takes place in 1850. Such distinction between the narration and the events it tells creates an inevitable distance between the reader and the Puritans because it is always offering an alternate system of values from the Puritans. Thus, the narrator can play off each age against the other. And in general, nineteenth-century values are shown as superior to Puritan ones, although the Puritans in some few ways were superior to the "present." But as much as he stresses difference and change, the narrator also never lets the reader forget that these Puritans were our ancestors, and that we live on the ground that they settled, within the institutions that they established. Thus, even though he separates us from the Puritans in one sense, he connects us very firmly to them in another.

One aspect of the narrator's nineteenth-century demeanor that would apear to contradict his narrative openness is his constant tendency to moralize. The flower that he offers at the beginning is a "sweet moral blossom," and the radiance of the supernatural *A* in the sky imparts a "moral interpretation" to the scene. Yet the contradiction is only apparent. At the same time that he insists that the world has or should have a moral interpretation, the narrator is carefully vague about what that interpretation should be. The moralizing is more rhetorical than substantive, a matter of good intentions more than of definite accomplishments. Such vagueness accords well with the desire to leave the story open rather than to close it within the confines of any single moral framework. In a sense, the moralism is "embroidery" on the fabric of the story; yet, just as Hester's embroidery of the letter cannot be separated from it, the moralism cannot be removed from *The Scarlet Letter.*

In Hawthorne's day many people were trying to separate morality from specific dogmas and doctrines, partly because the rapid proliferation of religious denominations in the United States threatened to create a kind of moral chaos, not to mention the real possibility of religious warfare. Americans could no longer afford to be intolerant. Thus, the idea of a transcendent morality, universal and attached to "our common nature" (55), emerged. Religion was losing its authority to legislate morality. The narrator's universal moral stance embodies such a nineteenth-century veiw of morality as transhistorical and transdoctrinal. Unity was increasingly to be a political matter, a question of the nation, rather than a religious one. The distinction that the Puritans did not recognize—between church and state—is a distinction on which *The Scarlet Letter* is morally based.

In addition, the "sweet moral blossom" is offered to "relieve" a story about "human frailty and sorrow," in terms that express compassion for human weakness rather than a judgment of human defectiveness. In fact, even to call a piece of moralism "sweet," or to imagine it as a "blossom," is to suggest that morality has a consolatory rather than a condemnatory role to play in human affairs. Along with his presentation of morality as something always and everywhere applicable, the narrator presents it as something sweet in and of itself.

Thus, we can make a few firm statements about the narrator's moral views, indeterminate as they generally are. No matter how he might sympathize with a given character's defiance of one or another particular, temporal, local formulation of a moral law, he would never accept a perspective that rejected the relevance of general moral categories for analyzing and understanding human life, as well as for making human life tolerable. In other words, morality should be a category of understanding rather than a basis for judgment and punishment. Moreover, as a category it must be grounded in the axiom that human nature, whatever it is, and in all its varieties, is common to all. The Puritans' worst fault, then, would have to be their exclusiveness; and yet this exclusiveness is precisely what had led them to the New World. The narrator is thus interpreting them against their own self-interpretation, performing an act that they would have rejected, that of integrating them into a view of common human nature.

3

WHO?
THE CHARACTERS

The "neutral territory" of Hawthorne's fiction serves the author's general goal of embodying his conviction that "reality," for all of us, is not a given something but is constructed by the interaction between our selective perceptions and what exists "out there." Some people are more objective than others, but nobody can attain a purely objective vision. Besides this general goal, the neutral territory provides Hawthorne with a fit habitat for a mix of characters, some fairly "realistic" in the way they are portrayed, others far more abstract or fantastic.

The cast of characters in *The Scarlet Letter* is quite small, and none of them is a wholly realistic character. The Puritans are portrayed as instances of a single type, not as individuals; Pearl and Chillingworth are developed as much for their symbolic values in relation to Hester and Dimmesdale, respectively, as they are for their own personalities; and even Dimmesdale and Hester are in part subjected to an allegorizing and typifying scheme. (Briefly, we can distinguish symbol from allegory by saying that a symbol attaches, by suggestion, a range of various abstract meanings to an object, while an allegory stands more forthrightly for a single idea. A character can be allegorical and symbolic simultaneously.) Every one of these personages would be out of place in the richly detailed and particularized world of a conventional realistic fiction. As Hawthorne himself described his practice, he kept the lights of his fiction dim so that these characters would seem life-like, knowing full well that in a bright glare they would fade away. Sometimes he regretted his inability to write purely realistic fiction: but he could not resist his own imaginative tendency to "embroider" a realistic scene with suggestions and implications.

THE PURITANS

The Puritan character is portrayed as a type in which all individuals in the Boston community participate, from the small children who play at going to church, scourging Quakers, and fighting Indians, through the pitiless chorus of women, and on to the authority figures of Governor Bellingham and Reverend Wilson. The very uniformity of this character is part of its nature—the Puritans are all alike and, taking themselves for the standard, see all difference and variety as unnatural, bad. To this sameness is added a quality that Hawthorne sometimes describes as the aptitude for reverence (237), and elsewhere as so strong a respect for authority and its forms that those forms are equated with the divine and the sacred (64). Since the Puritans revere authority, their authorities really are their representatives; and this is why the only developed Puritan characters in *The Scarlet Letter* are the rulers of church and state. The others are anonymous; the Puritan people as a whole are simply a crowd that Hawthorne calls on occasionally for general effect. It is significant, however, that the judgments of this crowd are frequently incorrect. Without directly saying that the rulers are wrong, the narrator can suggest that the elected representatives of people who are frequently mistaken may make mistakes themselves.

The rulers are described repeatedly with words like somber, wise, practical, hardheaded, unimaginative, unimpulsive, severe, stern, forceful, ponderous, martial, stately, weighty. They like ceremony, ritual, and shows of power. Toward the end of the book the narrator describes them as seldom brilliant, "but distinguished by a ponderous sobriety, rather than activity of intellect. They had fortitude and self-reliance, and, in time of difficulty or peril, stood up for the welfare of the state like a line of cliffs against a tempestuous tide" (238). Because they revere authority themselves, these men (they are all men) are dedicated to the welfare of the state. There certainly seems to be a degree of circularity here, the purpose of the state being nothing else than to establish itself; but we need to remember that Puritans thought of the state not as embodying their own character, but rather as articulating divine laws. In their role as creators and enforcers of the law they stand for, the rulers stand allegorically for law, authority, and power. Since they enforce law through display, they also stand for form and formality, as opposed to content and spontaneity.

With respect to their intention, which is to establish an enduring society, the Puritans must be judged successful—they have accomplished so much, the narrator remarks, precisely because they imagined and hoped so little (64). An important part of their character is their awareness of their own success, and their practical knowledge of what it takes to be successful. The Puritans value age and experience; there was no youth culture in early Boston. This preference explains why Hawthorne set his tale among the first generation, which was already mature at the time of the settlement.

For this group, the emigration to an unpeopled wilderness removes all impediments to the fullest development of their personal qualities. Anybody who does not fit the mold is punished or expelled. At the beginning of chapter 2 Hawthorne notes their ready reliance on public whippings for any number of reasons:

> It might be that a sluggish bond-servant, or an undutiful child, whom his parents had given over to the civil authority, was to be corrected at the whipping-post. It might be, that an Antinomian, a Quaker, or other heterodox religionist, was to be scourged out of the town, or an idle and vagrant Indian, whom the white man's fire-water had made riotous about the streets, was to be driven with stripes into the shadow of the forest. (49)

To a nineteenth-century audience, the narrator observes, some of these offenses would seem minor, but to a group that respects authority simply because it *is* authority, the breaking of any law is a matter of extreme seriousness, no matter which law it is.

Besides the frequency with which the Puritans punish, Hawthorne also stresses the attendant publicity. "A blessing on the righteous Colony of Massachusetts, where iniquity is dragged out into the sunshine! Come along, Madam Hester, and show your scarlet letter in the market-place!" (54). Because they are dedicated to forms, rules, laws, structures, the Puritans have no tolerance for secrets; they take people as purely public beings, and they hate and fear anything private. Their aim, insofar as their human subjects are concerned, is to turn anything private into something public. "It must gladden your heart," a man in the crowd says to Chillingworth, "to find yourself, at length, in a land where iniquity is searched out, and punished in the sight of rulers and people; as here in our godly New England" (62). For the Puritans, as Hawthorne portrays them, people are—or should be—all exterior, and as such there is nothing in them that is not appropriately subject to the state. We might go one step further and say, for the Puritans, people are entirely and only subjects.

The only apparent rift in Puritan uniformity is represented by Mistress Hibbins, the witch. The idea of witchcraft is the way in which the Puritans accommodate the inescapable reality, that people do have interior lives, into their worldview. Completely to deny an inescapable reality is to be mad, and the Puritans are anything but. Their solution—and how ingenious it is!—is to define the inner world as the most exterior world of all: as the alien world of the forest, the dark, the Black Man, the Other, something that comes upon them from the outside and tempts them away. The reversal of inside and outside is figured in some of the spatial ambiguities in Hawthorne's imagery: the forest, where the Black Man lives, seems both to surround, and to be surrounded by, the settlement.

Witchcraft, then, is a concept that the Puritans develop, and in this sense it is a fantasy, unreal. But it is a concept developed to take account of something that is real; and also, once developed, it takes on a life of its own. Thus, there are real witches in Puritan Boston, and the most notable of them is the governor's sister. Putting the witch and the governor in one house is a narrative economy and a great deal more besides. In the symbolic space of *The Scarlet Letter* Mistress Hibbins represents the other side of the coin of authority. The witches, who accept that they are evil and rejoice in their wickedness, have acquiesced in the Puritan worldview, and hence their actions are part of the foundations of Puritan authority. Witchcraft is not an accident or an aberration in the Puritan worldview; it is part of its essence. Hester—to jump ahead for a moment—refuses to join the witches because she will not accept an evaluation of her inner life as evil. In this respect she is truly aberrant whereas Mistress Hibbins is everything a witch should be.

PEARL

The character of Pearl is as much, or more, a symbolic function as she is the representation of a human child. In all the descriptions of Pearl, her affinity with the scarlet letter is stressed. She is its symbol, its double, its agent: "it was the scarlet letter in another form; the scarlet letter endowed with life!" (102). Hester carefully dresses Pearl in clothing that mimics the color and embroidery of the letter; this gesture also stresses the way in which the child is her mother's creation. As such, she is both something that the mother produces deliberately, and something that reflects the mother despite herself. More particularly, she reflects the mother's deed that gave her life (her life is never attributed to her father).

In one sense, the Puritan sense, that deed is equal to a broken law. "The child could not be made amenable to rules. In giving her existence, a great law had been broken; and the result was a being, whose elements were perhaps beautiful and brilliant, but all in disorder" (91). Hester recognizes in Pearl's character "the warfare" of her own spirit during the months when she was pregnant: "she could recognize her wild, desperate, defiant mood, the flightiness of her temper, and even some of the very cloud-shapes of gloom and despondency that had brooded in her heart" (91).

In another sense, however, the child is beauty and freedom and imagination and all the other natural qualities that the Puritan system denies. Beautiful, intelligent, perfectly shaped, vigorous, graceful, passionate, imaginative, impulsive, capricious, creative, visionary: these are only a sampling of the adjectives with which she is described. And these are all traits in Hester as well as in Pearl. Such descriptions suggest that Pearl is not an independent character so much as an abstraction of elements of Hester's character: a kind of "double," or "other self." This means that character analysis of Pearl is really analysis of Hester, and that the child's lawlessness shows how superficial Hester's quiet and subservient public demeanor is. And Hester's great love for the child signifies in part her refusal to disown her "sin" through a judgment that it was evil.

But Pearl is not simply a splitting off and intensifying of some aspects of Hester's character, a way of measuring Hester's attitudes. Quite apart from anything that Hester might intend consciously or unconsciously, Pearl seems to have a special, original relation to the letter. She is not only the letter as Hester might conceive it, but its agent in a scheme that is quite independent of her. If, in Hester's scheme, the child represents elements of defiant and lawless beauty, in this other scheme the child represents a form of conscience. It is her role to enforce the mother's guilt as well as to represent her rebellion. She does this simply by making it impossible for Hester to forget the letter. The letter is the first object that Pearl becomes aware of as a baby, and she keeps the letter firmly at the center of Hester's life by keeping it firmly in her infant regard. We see this role as enforcer of the letter most clearly in the forest scene, the one and only time that Hester throws the letter away. Oblivious to the mother's resurgent youth and beauty and happiness, Pearl refuses to join her until the letter is returned to its usual place. Only when she wears the letter is Hester her mother: and this, alas, is a true perception on Pearl's part. Should Hester repudiate the letter, she will repudiate Pearl.

Much in the depiction of Pearl is realistic; she is not all symbol and allegory. Hawthorne used his journal entries about his first child, Una, as sources for elements of his depiction of Pearl. Wildness, caprice, imaginativeness are all traits consistent with the nature of a young child who is endowed with energy and creativity and allowed a great deal of freedom. She lacks reference and adaptation to the world into which she was born, Hester thinks (91); but kept apart from society as Pearl is, any child would find it difficult to adapt.

If we could separate Pearl from her symbolic tasks in the novel, we might take her simply as an unusual (for its time), unidealized, and unsentimental description of a real child. Her attraction to the letter is easily explained: the letter is colorful and shiny. Her equation of it with her mother is likewise comprehensible: Pearl has never seen Hester without it. And as for her behavior in the forest, Hester herself offers the explanation that the child is jealous. Her reflecting of Hester's moods may have nothing mysterious about it: spending so much time with her mother, being completely dependent on her, and possessing an imaginative nature, Pearl would naturally be keenly attuned to Hester, even more than the preoccupied mother might be herself. Pearl's extreme restlessness during the last scene in the marketplace, the narrator says, was "played upon and vibrated with her mother's disquietude" (244).

However realistic she may be, there is no mistaking that at the end of the book (when she kisses her father) Pearl becomes fully human for the first time. "A spell was broken. The great scene of grief, in which the wild infant bore a part, had developed all her sympathies; and as her tears fell upon her father's cheek, they were the pledge that she would grow up amid human joy and sorrow, not for ever do battle with the world, but be a woman in it. Towards her mother, too, Pearl's errand as a messenger of anguish was all fulfilled" (256). So Pearl has been the letter's messenger (its angel, in the word's original sense) and the letter's incarnation; and she has also been its victim. Her victimization has consisted in being denied a reality of her own. At the very moment when she becomes real, nevertheless—when her errand toward Hester is fulfilled—she ceases to be a character in the story. Thus, the human character Pearl is not really part of *The Scarlet Let-*

ter, and the character in the book is best thought of as a symbol and a function who is "naturalized" by being given a smattering of realistic traits.

Hawthorne's choice of humanizing event for Pearl should not go unremarked, however. She is initiated into humanity by participating in a "great scene of grief," whose result is both to learn who her father is (a question, curiously, that she has never asked in so many words) and to lose him. We might say, she learns who her father *was*. If this plot invention tells us anything about what Hawthorne thinks it means to be human, it is not that (as the Puritans would see it) humanity is rooted in evil, but that it is rooted in loss. In this connection we can observe that there are no families in *The Scarlet Letter.* The society is full of patriarchs, authorities, rulers, and father figures, but it is devoid of real fathers. The founding "fathers" are oddly unfamilial, and Dimmesdale, who wants so badly to be one of them, must pay for membership in the ruling group by absenting himself from the lives of both Hester and Pearl. It could be argued that the strongest positive emotional weight in the story is attached neither to the mother-child couple nor to the woman-man couple, but to the triangulation of the three people as a nuclear family—except that, Hawthorne seems to suggest, the soil of New England is not congenial to this triangle. Why should this be? Because the idealized, loving family cannot exist in a society where people are merely subjects for authority. In that society fathers are only figures.

CHILLINGWORTH

Many critics over the years have been fascinated by the psychology of Roger Chillingworth, but structually he is a character of the same type as Pearl, chiefly symbolic and allegorical. As Mistress Hibbins and Governor Bellingham are identified as parts of a whole by being made to live together in the same house, as Pearl lives with Hester, so Chillingworth lives with Dimmesdale and can be thought of as a part of him. Just as Hester can be better understood by analyzing Pearl, Dimmesdale can be better understood by analyzing Chillingworth.

Pearl and Chillingworth both, from different perspectives, stand for the Broken Law. And the differences between Dimmesdale and Hester can be seen most intensely in a contrast of their constant companions.

To be sure, some space is devoted to the idea of a deterioration and change in Chillingworth, as though he were a realistic character. But the change is always described in highly fanciful language. Although some of that language comes from the superstitious multitude, their explanations are replicated in the narrator's metaphors. Thus, "according to the vulgar idea, the fire in his laboratory had been brought from the lower regions, and was fed with infernal fuel; and so, as might be expected, his visage was getting sooty with the smoke" (127). This medieval representation of Chillingworth's alteration is validated, only two pages later, by the narrator, who says, in language equally fanciful, that "sometimes, a light glimmered out of the physican's eyes, burning blue and ominous, like the reflection of a furnace, or . . . one of those gleams of ghastly fire that darted from Bunyan's awful doorway in the hill-side" (129). The only way that we can allow that there really was a blue light burning out of Chillingworth's eyes is to allow him a nonrealistic level of existence in the story.

In a later chapter Hester looks at Chillingworth and observes from his changed appearance that he has become a fiend. The narrator corroborates her reading:

> Old Roger Chillingworth was a striking evidence of man's faculty of transforming himself into a devil, if he will only, for a reasonable space of time, undertake a devil's office. This unhappy person had effected such a transformation by devoting himself, for seven years, to the constant analysis of a heart full of torture, and deriving his enjoyment thence, and adding fuel to those fiery tortures which he analyzed and gloated over. (170).

Materializing out of the forest, realistically explained as Hester's husband, Chillingworth quickly loses his human identity and, attaching himself to the minister, begins his mission—like Pearl's, that of "a messenger of anguish." He becomes the extremest representation possible of a pitiless conscience, and well suggests the idea that no judge is so exacting as the judge within. "All that guilty sorrow, hidden from the world, whose great heart would have pitied and forgiven, to be revealed to him, the Pitiless, to him, the Unforgiving!" (139). If Pearl is not yet human, Chillingworth is no longer human, and after Dimmesdale's death "he positively withered up, shrivelled away, and almost vanished from mortal sight, like an uprooted weed that lies wilting in the sun" (260).

Also, along with his role as Dimmesdale's alter ego, Chillingworth has a story of his own. Those who have read Hawthorne's better-known short works will recall how often he wrote allegories about people with obsessions, people who become their own victims. Quite often, these obsessed people start out as particularly rational, even scientific, individuals. They are overtaken by their goals; they lose touch with humanity; they become monsters; and they often end up as destroyers of those they love. In fact, as Hawthorne's stories tend to represent it, those who are obsessed have become incapable of love; perhaps their original weakness is a dearth of human connection in the first place. At some level all obsession is self-obsession, hence egoism and obsession are the same. (Some examples of such stories are "Ethan Brand," "Rappaccini's Daughter," "The Birthmark," "The Great Carbuncle," "The Man of Adamant," and "Egotism; or, The Bosom Serpent.")

Certainly, Hawthorne locates Chillingworth's susceptibility to obsession in his original lack of warmth. This lack of warmth is both the cause of, and is augmented by, his occupation as a scientist and a scholar. The scientist has a mentality prone to dispassionate experimentation. But after banishing his passions, he finds them returning as obsessions. The scholar tends to substitute books for life, perhaps because his capacity for life is weak.

Interestingly, in view of the fact that Hawthorne was himself a writer of books and an avid reader, not one reference to books and learning in *The Scarlet Letter* is favorable. The Bible, as noted earlier, is virtually unmentioned, and the book most often referred to is its antithesis, the book carried under the Devil's arm, wherein he writes the names of those who join his satanic society. Otherwise, a life among books is seen as cause or result of a lack of capacity for fellowship: Reverend Wilson looks like a frontispiece in a volume of sermons, and has "no more right than one of those portraits would have, to step forth, as he now did, and meddle with a question of human guilt, passion, and anguish" (65). Chillingworth explains his inadequacies as Hester's huband by calling himself "the book-worm of great libraries" (74). Though one person can be both scientist and scholar, there is a difference between them. The scholar tends to be conservative and traditional, the scientist is more radical in thought and temperament. The scholar looks backward: the scientist, forward. But neither of them relates to the moment; like Pearl, they lack reference and adaptation to the world in which they were born.

Thus, if we know Hawthorne's previous writings, we are not surprised that he embodies his figure of obsessive vengeance in a scientist and scholar. Nor that Chillingworth's investigation, undertaken "with the severe and equal integrity of a judge, desirous only of truth," quickly gives way to "a terrible fascination, a kind of fierce, though still calm, necessity," which seizes him and never sets him free again (129). New to Hawthorne's treatment of this type in *The Scarlet Letter* is his developing of the character in connection with the Broken Law, thereby making him a metaphoric judge, a law enforcer.

HESTER

In Hester Prynne, Hawthorne created the first true heroine of American fiction, as well as one of its enduring heroes. Hester is a heroine because she is deeply implicated in, and responsive to, the gender structure of her society, and because her story, turning on "love," is "appropriate" for a woman. She is a hero because she has qualities and actions that transcend this gender reference and lead to heroism as it can be understood for anyone.

"Such helpfulness was found in her,—so much power to do, and power to sympathize,—that many people refused to interpret the scarlet *A* by its original signification. They said that it meant Able; so strong was Hester Prynne, with a woman's strength" (161). "Neither can I any longer live without her companionship; so powerful is she to sustain,—so tender to soothe!" (201). It is impossible to miss, in these and many other passages, the stress on Hester's remarkable strength as well as the fundamentally humane uses to which she puts it. Without going beyond the license that Hawthorne allows, one might allegorize Hester as Good Power, which is, after all, precisely what, in the basic structural scheme of all narrative, one looks for in a hero. The power is remarkable in that its existence seems so improbable in an outcast woman. If the Puritan state draws its power from the consensual community and the laws that uphold it, then clearly Hester has access to a completely different source of power— or is, perhaps, herself an alternative source of power. And it is a power that even the Puritan world cannot deny, for "with her native energy of character, and rare capacity, it could not entirely cast her off" (84).

Perhaps, however, it is precisely her essential alienation from the community that explains this power. Although Hester can hardly doubt the power of the Puritan community to punish her and define the circumstances of her life, she knows—as we do—that they have this power only because she has granted it to them. She is free to leave Boston whenever she chooses. Her decision to stay entails a submission to Puritan power, but since she can withdraw her consent at any time this submission is always provisional. Her reasons for staying may be misguided, but they are her own. In schematic terms, if the Puritans symbolize the law, then Hester symbolizes the individual person—with this important proviso: she also symbolizes good. It would be easy to deduce from this polarity that Hawthorne wants us to think that law is bad and the individual good—but that would be too easy. Matters in Hawthorne are never so clear-cut. But he certainly gives us a situation wherein two kinds of power confront each other in conflict, and strongly suggests that any society that regards the power of the individual only as an adversary to be overcome, is profoundly defective and deeply inhuman.

Hester's situation, even before the commission of her "sin," is that of an outsider. She was sent to Massachusetts in advance of her husband; he had decided to emigrate, not she. The native strength of her character is certainly abetted by the fact that, as a young woman in a society dominated by aging men, she has no public importance. Even when she becomes a public figure through her punishment, her psyche is largely left alone. The magistrates condemn her to wear the letter but thereafter seem to have only a very superficial interest in her. A minister who sees her on the street may take the opportunity to preach an extempore sermon; people stare at the letter; children jeer; but none of this behavior represents an attempt to change Hester's mind. It is hoped that the external letter will work its way down into Hester's heart and cause repentance, but nobody really cares and this indifference is Hester's freedom. In fact, the effect of the letter so far as Hester's character is concerned is the opposite of what was intended: turning her into a public symbol, it conceals her individuality and thus protects it.

As the representative of individuality, Hester, rather than subjecting herself to the law, subjects it to her own scrutiny; as I have said, she takes herself as a law. She is not, by nature, rebellious; and during the seven-year period of *The Scarlet Letter*'s action, she certainly attempts to accept the judgment implicit in the letter. If she could accept that judgment she would be able to see purpose and meaning in her suffering. But ultimately she is unable to transcend her heartfelt conviction that she has not sinned. She loves Dimmesdale, with whom she sinned; she loves the child that her sin brought forth. How, then, can she agree that her deed was wrong?

She goes so far in her thinking as to attribute her own law to God, thus denying the entire rationale of the Puritan community, their certainty that their laws conform to divine intention. "Man had marked this woman's sin by a scarlet letter, which had such potent and disastrous efficacy that no human sympathy could reach her, save it were sinful like herself. God, as a direct consequence of the sin which man thus punished, had given her a lovely child, whose place was on that same dishonored bosom, to connect her parent for ever with the race and descent of mortals, and to be finally a blessed soul in heaven!" (89).

In fact, while the outward Hester performs deeds of mercy and kindness throughout the seven years, the inward Hester grows ever more alienated and over time becomes—what she was not at first—a genuine revolutionary and social radical.

> The world's law was no law for her mind. It was an age in which the human intellect, newly emancipated, had taken a more active and a wider range than for many centuries before. Men of the sword had overthrown nobles and kings. Men bolder than these had overthrown and rearranged—not actually, but within the sphere of theory, which was their most real abode—the whole system of ancient prejudice, wherewith was linked much of ancient principle. Hester Prynne imbibed this spirit. She assumed a freedom of speculation, then common enough on the other side of the Atlantic, but which our forefathers, had they known of it, would have held to be a deadlier crime than that stigmatized by the scarlet letter. (164)

Had she spoken her thoughts, she probably would "have suffered death from the stern tribunals of the period, for attempting to undermine the foundations of the Puritan establishment" (165). If it were not for the existence of Pearl, for whose sake she lives quietly in Boston, she would have become, like Anne Hutchinson, a religious reformer.

But just as Hester refuses to take the road to witchcraft on account of Pearl, she rejects Hutchinson's radical path for the same reason. She feels particular obligations to human beings far more than she feels general social responsibilities. She behaves as a sister of mercy in the community because this is the way to live unmolested, not because she believes in doing good. And she wants to live unmolested so that she can bring up Pearl. Staying in Boston on account of Dimmesdale, and living there as she does on account of Pearl, Hester's behavior is appropriate to her role as representative of individual and personal, rather than social, power. A reformer is dedicated to social power and has abandoned an individual center. No doubt this makes the whole issue of social reform on behalf of individualism highly problematic; so far as Hester is concerned—and this is our concern at present—the very consistency of her individualism keeps her within the sphere of the personal. At the end of the story, with her group of women clustered about her, she invokes the memory of Hutchinson only to contrast with it. The subject of talk among the women is entirely personal, centered on secular love; Hester counsels patience. Thus, the narrator's suggestion that her radicalism stems from an unquiet heart is partly validated by her behavior. If in Hawthorne's world a true radical, motivated by the impersonal, is somehow anti-individual, and if a true individual, motivated by the personal, is ultimately not radical, then our current popular understanding of these terms is quite different from Hawthorne's. His distinction is between ideologues and individuals rather than between varieties of ideology: an "individual-ist" is an ideologue. The individual as a reality rather than a concept is always extremely vulnerable.

Among Hester's key defining traits we cannot overlook her "skill at her needle." If her nature includes the characters of outcast, rebel, lover, mother, and sister of mercy, it also includes the character of artist. Her gift for needlework is the expression of an artist's nature; the embroideries that she produces are genuine works of art.

We meet her skill first, of course, in the letter, which, "surrounded with an elaborate embroidery and fantastic flourishes of gold thread," is "so artistically done, and with so much fertility and gorgeous luxuriance of fancy, that it had all the effect of a last and fitting decoration" to her splendid apparel (53). Hester's grand costuming for the scaffold scene, far more elegant than what the dress code of the colony normally would allow her, is not seen again. She wears nothing but drab gray gowns. Her dreary dress, however, becomes a frame for the letter, and the letter remains, as it is clearly meant to be, an ornament. Beautifying the letter through art is another way in which Hester breaks the Puritan law (although the Puritan rulers—unlike the women in the crowd—are too literal-minded to notice it). The letter becomes the chief ground for the struggle between Hester and the

Puritans, and it is able to play this role because of Hester's gift as an artist.

It is tempting here to associate artistic skill with social rebellion, but the equation does not hold. For Hester supports herself in Puritan Boston chiefly by making the elaborate decorative garments that the magistrates wear for public occasions and that are allowed to the better-off in the colony. "Deep ruffs, painfully wrought bands, and gorgeously embroidered gloves, were all deemed necessary to the official state of men assuming the reins of power; and were readily allowed to individuals dignified by rank or wealth" (82). Art does not have an inherently political nature, although—as the instance of the letter shows—it can become highly politicized. Rather, it is the expression of an original and creative energy, of fertility, of imagination, and of the love for the beautiful, even the gorgeous. This energy and creativity have no reference to society at all. Artists and their products can be appropriated by society or condemned by it; but society cannot make art, only individuals can. Indeed, only individuals who retain, or contain, a profound nonsocial element in their makeup (as Hester does) can make art. Although the social structure of the age denies virtually all forms of artistic expression to women, it does allow this one, and Hester makes use of it as an outlet for this side of her nature. For its part, society makes use of *her*. The Puritans may be incapable of producing art, but they certainly want to possess it. Therefore, despite everything, they want Hester in their community; and they want her *as she is*. But this is something they have to learn about themselves; and if they do not learn in time, there will be a society with no more Hesters.

DIMMESDALE

Each character in *The Scarlet Letter* has a function in the plot, and each relates to all the others in an abstract pattern of contrast and doubling. Chillingworth doubles Dimmesdale's conscience, but contrasts with him as a scientist to a scholar. Pearl doubles Hester's creativity and beauty, but her anarchic freedom contrasts with Hester's continuous self-control. Mistress Hibbins, in principle the Puritans' opposite, doubles the vision of evil that they have created. And so on. Dimmesdale, as the partner of Hester's sin and yet a person affected by it in a completely different way, is chiefly developed by Hawthorne as a contrast with and comparison to the heroine. While she is unable, in her heart, to think of their act as evil, he is equally incapable of thinking of it as good. While on the outside Hester is a branded, shamed woman, on the inside she is independent and free. Dimmesdale, externally independent and free, is internally branded and shamed. She is a social outcast, he a pillar of society. Above all, her deed is expressed and his is hidden.

At the same time that Hawthorne develops Dimmesdale's character and situation with continual reference to Hester, he gives Dimmesdale's portrait a rich psychological texture that makes him, for many, as interesting in himself as Hester. For some, he is even more interesting. Certainly, he is a more troubled and divided character than Hester, whose strength and consistency produce a certain uniformity and predictability of effect.

The chief key to Dimmesdale's character is not his religious piety but his dependence on the good opinion of society. He is a "true religionist, with the reverential sentiment largely developed, and an order of mind that impelled itself powerfully along the track of a creed, and wore its passage continually deeper with the lapse of time. In no state of society would he have been what is called a man of liberal views; it would always be essential to his peace to feel the pressure of a faith about him, supporting, while it confined him within its iron framework" (123). It is above all Hester's ability to stand alone that distinguishes her from him; he needs support and confinement.

Given this need, Dimmesdale is not a person who can easily hold a view contrary to society's, even when society's view leads to self-condemnation. He never doubts for an instant that what he and Hester did in the forest was evil. He never doubts that he deserves to be punished. But to confess his act and receive the punishment that would satisfy his sense of guilt would be to lose his position in society, which he cannot live without. Thus, the very social dependency that makes him condemn himself also keeps him from confessing. He is doubly split: between his outer and inner selves, and within his inner self as well.

As a means of equivocating between mutually incompatible psychic demands, Dimmesdale engages in all sorts of fakeries. He carries out a variety of private penances: fasting, flagellation, nights without sleep. But these activities are no substitute for the public confession that he knows his sin requires; thus, they are decadent self-indulgences. He does confess publicly time after time, but always in a symbolic language that he knows will be misunderstood. On each such occasion he enjoys the combined relief of venting the truth while staving off an irreversible self-exposure, all the while suffering from his own contemptuous self-estimate.

> The minister well knew—subtle, but remorseful hypocrite that he was!—the light in which his vague confession would be viewed. He had striven to put a cheat upon himself by making the avowal of a guilty conscience, but had gained only one other sin, and a self-acknowledged shame, without the momentary relief of being self-deceived. He had spoken the very truth, and transformed it into the veriest falsehood. And yet, by the constitution of his nature, he loved the truth, and loathed the lie, as few men ever did. Therefore, above all things else, he loathed his miserable self! (144)

If Dimmesdale were merely a social parasite or a clever charlatan, he would not be an object of compassion, as he seems clearly meant to be. Though he lacks Hester's courage and fortitude, he has other inherently valuable qualities: sensitivity, intelligence, kindness, benevolence, the desire to do good, the love of truth, and a basic unworldliness that contrasts attractively with the hard practicality of the other Puritan leaders. The hypocrisy in which he is involved, however, alienates him from his own goodness. In contrast to Hester, who is always real and substantial and never loses touch with her own essence, he becomes progressively more unreal to himself. "To the untrue man, the whole universe is false,—it is impalpable,—it shrinks to nothing within his grasp. And he himself, in so far as he shows himself in a false light, becomes a shadow, or, indeed, ceases to exist" (145–46).

Part of Dimmesdale's agony during these years comes directly from his increasing abilities as a minister. He becomes a wonderful preacher and an effective counselor. It seems that sin has made him better suited for his work, a strange and distressing discovery for one who has carefully kept himself apart from the world precisely to preserve his purity. As a Hawthorne Puritan, Dimmesdale cannot explain a connection between his "fall" and his success except as a sign of his enlistment in the devil's party. He has rationalized his failure to confess by telling himself that his congregation needs him—how can they need someone doing the devil's work? A strenuous argument on just this point occurs between Dimmesdale and Chillingworth in chapter 10. "Woulds't thou have me to believe, O wise and pious friend, that a false show can be better—can be more for God's glory, or man's welfare—than God's own truth? Trust me, such men deceive themselves!" Chillingworth exclaims (133). If Chillingworth is wrong, the entire social structure may rest on a foundation of evil. This is the position that Dimmesdale's rationalizing leads to.

In his analysis of Dimmesdale Hawthorne shows keen insight into disordered mental states. "The only truth, that continued to give Mr. Dimmesdale a real existence on this earth, was the anguish in his inmost soul, and the undissembled expression of it in his aspect. Had he once found power to smile, and wear a face of gayety, there would have been no such man!" (146). In a sense, Dimmesdale's struggle for seven years is, quite literally, to keep body and soul together, by allowing some external sign of his inner state to be visible. His face, reflecting his torment, constitutes such a sign. So too—although it is not yet publicly visible—does the emerging letter on his chest.

It is no wonder, then, that after his climactic encounter with Hester in the forest, Dimmesdale goes briefly insane, if by insanity we mean the total collapse of a whole self. Hester, who has meant to save him—whom he has implored to save him—cannot do so; her truth is not his truth. Leaving the forest after having experienced what he interprets as a new birth, Dimmesdale certainly does smile and wear a face of gaiety; and thereby, exactly as Hawthorne predicted, he ceases to exist. Of course, flight to Europe with Hester and Pearl is altogether unthinkable. He could never live that way. But having given himself over to the concept of flight and freedom, he can no longer live in duplicity, either. With a kind of superhuman effort, he diverts his mad energy to one crowning achievement, and preaches the greatest—and the last—sermon of his life.

Is his motive in the sermon the desire to serve God, or is it simply one more expression of his egoism? One aspect of the minister's ceaseless brooding on his own sin is the self-absorption it implies. Dimmesdale is clearly obsessed with his secret just as much as Chillingworth is. And what are the motives behind his final confession on the scaffold? Is this not yet another exhibition of self? Keeping his secret means that Dimmesdale can never acknowledge Hester or Pearl. Twentieth-century readers are apt to take very seriously his failure to accept his responsibilities toward his "family," all the more when this failure is contrasted to Hester's behavior. It would be gratifying, therefore, if his final confession on the scaffold could be read as a belated avowal of his human ties to them. But if his calling Hester and Pearl to the scaffold with him has such a meaning, it is also part of a drama staged to allot him the central role. Speaking of himself in the third person, Dimmesdale cries, "He bids you look again at Hester's scarlet letter! He tells you, that, with all its mysterious horror, it is but the shadow of what he bears on his own breast, and that even this, his own red stigma, is no more than the type of what has seared his inmost heart!" (255). Hester's suffering is appropriated to his own use, made into a pale duplicate and sign of his infinitely greater suffering.

Dimmesdale, as noted, is not a truly religious man in the sense of one who really believes the tenets of the religion he practices. He is religious because of his dependent and praise-requiring temperament. Hawthorne seems almost to suggest that Dimmesdale stands for all religious people, that faith is a matter of psychological need, not of necessary truth. Such a suggestion fits in with the universalizing morality we have observed to be at work in the novel. Another way of understanding Hawthorne's strategy here, however, is as a refusal to use the novel as a forum for discussing religious truth at all. Remember that this is called not a tale of human sin and redemption, but one of frailty and sorrow.

The biographical Hawthorne's own religious views have proven extremely difficult to clarify. As a child he went to church with his mother and aunts, or heard the Bible read at his grandmother's. In college he was required to take Bible study class and attend Sunday sermons, which were of the hellfire and brimstone variety. Subsequently, he never attended a church service or even entered a church except as a sightseer in Europe. Allusions to religion that can be extracted from his journals, his letters, and the reminiscences of his friends and acquaintances are few and thoroughly conventional. Guilt—that is, a subjective feeling—rather than sin—that is, an objective reality—was the focus of his investigation in Dimmesdale's case.

And even Dimmesdale's guilt is depicted in terms of his alienation from his own center and from society, whereas the real psychology of a religious being would probably have a different focus. A religious person who believed himself a sinner would surely be deeply, even obsessively, concerned with his relation to God; but this seems to be the least of Dimmesdale's worries. Indeed, he rebukes Chillingworth for seeking to thrust himself between "the sufferer and his God" (137), as though this was the one secure and untouchable area of his life. It would seem that Hawthorne's reluctance to deal with religious issues goes so far as to make him draw back from portraying the psychology of a deeply religious man. Hawthorne has carefully drawn his boundaries and never oversteps them. The matter for fiction is wide-ranging; yet Hawthorne, while expanding the range of the novel through the material he treated in *The Scarlet Letter,* was not willing to venture into theology.

HAWTHORNE AS PSYCHOLOGIST

An examination of characters in *The Scarlet Letter* would not be complete if it did not stress Hawthorne's contribution to psychological understanding. Even though the book often introduces allegorical or partly allegorical characters, and depends on old-fashioned personifications and other techniques to bring out inner truths, the very fact that it is concerned with *inner* truth puts it at the forefront of the development of psychological fiction. In his recognition of the hidden life and his description of mental processes Hawthorne was a psychologist ahead of his time.

Psychological speculation is as old as Aristotle, but the idea of a scientific, analytic psychology was new in the nineteenth century, and there did not yet exist the rich array of concepts, the wide vocabulary, and the accumulation of data that would later develop. This is why Hawthorne was apt to depend on outmoded literary techniques for representing some of his insights into mental states and processes. Moreover, since science in his time was intensely materialistic in its approach, he probably meant to suggest, by using old-fashioned rhetoric, that some important human truths known to earlier generations had been lost sight of in the positivist intellectual orientation of contemporary scientific thought. For such an implication, outdated language and techniques would be quite fitting.

Even so, however, certain elements of the psychological representation in *The Scarlet Letter* are strikingly innovative and advanced, and liable to be overlooked if we succumb entirely to the novel's intentional archaisms. For example, it is an advanced idea to split the inner life fundamentally from the outer, as Hawthorne does in the cases of Hester and Dimmesdale, and at the same time to place the key to identity in the thoughts, emotions, and fantasies of these characters rather than in their behavior. Today this idea is commonplace; in Hawthorne's time it was not, and the novel as a genre was taking the lead in investigating the "interior of a heart," as Hawthorne's chapter title describes it. The vast increase in awareness of, and attention to, the interior world was an offshoot of the general romantic movement with its tremendous focus on the single self. Among intellectual forms, fiction was especially well suited to treat the concept in depth and with detailed examples.

But along with a stress on the mental life of his major characters, which he shares with many other novelists of his time, Hawthorne offers us other, more personal psychological insights. He suggests the existence, not exactly of a single, unified unconscious as Freud was to hypothesize, but certainly of continual unconscious thought processes, with accompanying defenses and rationalizations on the part of the conscious mind as it seeks to contain while pretending not to know its deeper layers. The usually hidden unconscious becomes visible in periods of mental conflict, and also in states of unusual excitement. Important scenes in *The Scarlet Letter* show Hester or Dimmesdale at such times.

The first episode of extreme mental stimulation occurs at the beginning of the story when Hester is exposed on the scaffold. After describing her from the outside, as she appeared to the Puritan multitude and as she might have appeared to a cultural outsider, the narrator moves into her mind and follows her own currents of thought. "Her mind, and especially her memory, was preternaturally active, and kept bringing up other scenes than this . . . one picture precisely as vivid as another; as if all were of similar importance, or all alike a play. Possibly, it was an instinctive device of her spirit, to relieve itself, by the exhibition of these phantasmagoric forms, from the cruel weight and hardness of the reality" (57). Here Hester's mind seems out of control, or rather the conscious mind is simply a screen on which another, deeper mind (an "instinctive device of her spirit") is casting its images; at times of enormous stress, the controlling mind gives way to reveal the presence of layers of usually obscured or—to use a modern term—repressed mental activity.

As a character distinguished, however, by striking self-control, Hester does not often succumb to eruptions of the unconscious in this manner. Her conscious mind is occupied nonetheless with excluding unacceptable thoughts from its precincts. In devoting so much of her needlecraft to creating "coarse garments for the poor," the narrator suggests, "it is probable that there was an idea of penance," which, however, was "morbid," betokening "something doubtful, something that might be deeply wrong, beneath" (83–84). The word *beneath* here divides the mind into layers, and identifies the center of the psyche not in surface rationality but in the hidden desires beneath, thus portioning mental life into conscious and unconscious layers, as Freud was to do half a century later.

Earlier in this same chapter Hawthorne has attempted to explain why, "with the world before her," Hester chose to stay in Boston, and here he distinguishes even more carefully between surface explanation—what the mind tells itself—and "true" explanation, which, because it doesn't suit one's self-image, the mind rejects. "It might be, too—doubtless it was so, although she hid the secret from herself, and grew pale whenever it struggled out of her heart, like a serpent from its hole,—it might be that another feeling kept her. . . . She barely looked the idea in the face, and hastened to bar it in its dungeon. What she compelled herself to believe,—what, finally, she reasoned upon, as her motive for continuing a resident of New England,—was half a truth, and half a self-delusion" (80). What is this idea, this feeling? Simply that she continues to love Dimmesdale and to hope that somehow circumstances will bring them together. This is one of the striking early instances in literature of the depiction of the mind as a divided space, and of the processes of rationalization that impose a spurious wholeness on it.

Another occurs later on, after Hester has spoken with Chillingworth about her decision to break her vow of secrecy. Hester has previously constructed for herself a noble—which is to say, unselfish—explanation of the act she has decided to perform: "Hester could not but ask herself, whether there has not originally been a defect of truth, courage, and loyalty, on her own part, in allowing the minister to be thrown into a position where so much evil was to be foreboded. . . . She determined to redeem her error, so far as it might yet be possible" (166–67). Nobody can disapprove, after all, of an act motivated by the desire to be true, courageous, and loyal.

But after her interview with Chillingworth, Hester finds her mind in a turmoil, and other motives come to the surface: her lively hatred of Chillingworth for having betrayed her into loveless marriage and cheated her of deserved happiness, for one; her continued love for Dimmesdale; her living desire, despite everything, for an intimacy with him. "The emotions of that brief space . . . threw a dark light on Hester's state of mind, revealing much that she might not otherwise have acknowledged to herself" (177). Yet even as hidden emotions come to the attention of the conscious mind, they continue to evade its control. For the first time since putting on the letter Hester lies about it and grows harshly defensive with Pearl; and, the narrator comments, such behavior suggests that perhaps "some new evil had crept" into her heart, "or some old one had never been expelled" (181). When Hester, her patience at an end, threatens to shut Pearl in the dark closet, she is expressing in outward behavior the mental gesture of denying or suppressing the feelings that have revealed themselves to her—shutting them away with Pearl in the dark closet. The heart, as Hawthorne tells us often in his allegorical figures, is a cave or cellar where corpses have been buried, a closet where evil thoughts have been discarded. It is not only, as optimistic Americans would prefer to believe, the source of a fountain of pure feeling and innocent goodness.

With Dimmesdale, whose mind is more fragile and more badly divided than Hester's, Hawthorne can more fully elaborate this model of the inner world. Dimmesdale, it might be said, operates in a continual state of extreme excitement; this is what is killing him. His regular fasting induces hallucinatory states: "his brain often reeled, and visions seemed to flit before him"—devils, angels, the dead friends of his youth, his parents, Hester and Pearl. These visions were, the narrator remarks, "in one sense, the truest and most substantial things which the poor minister now dealt with" (145).

Yet even in his keyed-up existence there are peaks of much greater agitation—in particular, his secret penance on the scaffold (chapter 12, "The Minister's Vigil") and his return from the forest after meeting Hester (chapter 20, "The Minister in a Maze"). In both episodes the minister's conscious mind becomes a passive receiver for images and impulses projected from lower mental depths. And in both, the images express a counterforce to the minister's continual effort to be good, to be perfect, to be better than anybody else has ever been; they reveal all the contrary impulses to be what we might today call "normal." Dimmesdale interprets these impulses as evidence of evil, and we must interpret their eruption at the least as psychological breakdown.

On the scaffold (chapter 12), Dimmesdale actually delights in the possibility that he may be discovered, even while, as the narrator comments, his behavior is a mockery, "in which his soul trifled with itself" (148). As was the case with Hester on the scaffold earlier, the organizing power of the conscious mind, its ability to discriminate between inner and outer, important and trivial, disappears: watching an approaching light, Dimmesdale sees it shine on a post, a garden fence, a pump, a water trough, an oak door, an iron knocker, noticing "all these minute particulars, even while firmly convinced that the doom of his existence was stealing onward" (149–50). As the night wears on, he comes close to hallucinating, in a phantasmagoric scene wherein the whole town rises up at dawn and comes running out to see him on the scaffold: patriarchs in their nightgowns, Governor Bellingham with his ruff askew, and the young virgins of his parish who had made a shrine for Dimmesdale in their "white bosoms; which, now, by the by, in their hurry and confusion, they would scantly have given themselves time to cover with their kerchiefs" (151–52). Dimmesdale's desire to mock the decorum of the elders is expressed in his disrespectful images of their disarray; and his suppressed sexuality turns the young women of his parish into half-clothed groupies. His unconscious mind relieves itself in irreverent and disruptive jokes.

This episode comes to a climax with the appearance of a comet in the sky, whose eerie light shows "the familiar scene of the street, with the distinctness of mid-day, but also with the awfulness that is always imparted to familiar objects by an unaccustomed light" (154). Here three interpretive modes converge: a naturalistic interpretation, in which the comet simply appears when it appears for reasons having to do with the movement of heavenly bodies; a social interpretation, whereby the Puritans together find a meaning in the comet pertinent to their "infant commonwealth"; and a private interpretation, with

Dimmesdale assuming that the A-shaped comet has appeared especially as a message for him. Such an interpretation, according to the
narrator, could "only be the symptom of a highly disordered mental
state, when a man, rendered morbidly self-contemplative by long, intense, and secret pain, had extended his egotism over the whole ex-
panse of nature, until the firmament itself should appear no more than
a fitting page for his soul's history and fate" (154–55). The narrator
prefigures here the condition that we would today call paranoia, the
outward projection of obsession.

The same processes are at work again in the scene of Dimmesdale's
return from the forest; once more he is the passive and almost helpless
spectator of his own forbidden and threatening impulses. This is a
much more dramatic scene than the meditation on the scaffold, for the
minister has now taken a conscious, willful step toward rebellion. He
is beset by appalling temptations. "At every step he was incited to do
some strange, wild, wicked thing or other, with a sense that it would
be at once involuntary and intentional; in spite of himself, yet growing
out of a profounder self than that which opposed the impulse" (217).
These desires, willed but resisted, recognized but denied, have an obvious aspect of disruptive humor about them, a wish to mock the pu-
ritanical code and his own submission to it. Dimmesdale wants to
make blasphemous suggestions to an elderly, respectable deacon and
a devout old widow; to make a lewd proposal to a young and beautiful parishioner; to teach dirty words to children; to trade obscene
jokes with a sailor.

Yet if these impulses are funny and, to a twentieth-century mind,
rather pathetic than wicked, there is no doubt that their emergence is
not a sign of the minister's having won his emotional and mental freedom but rather of his near approach to mental breakdown. To recognize divisions and conflicts in the mind, the presence of the
repressed, the power of the unconscious, is not necessarily to become
an advocate of what, in the twentieth century, we might call "sincerity" or "authenticity." Nor does the narrator suggest that the newly
revealed impulses are expressions of Dimmesdale's essential and natural goodness; on the contrary, he says firmly that these impulses rep-

resent "scorn, bitterness, unprovoked malignity, gratuitous desire of ill, ridicule of whatever was good and holy" (222).

Examining Dimmesdale's hypocrisy in refusing to confess his sin, Hawthorne relies, just as he did in showing Hester's denied yet overwhelming passion for Dimmesdale, on concepts of such mental processes as self-delusion and rationalization. Dimmesdale justifies his silence to himself chiefly on altruistic grounds: he wishes to do good for his congregation and would lose this ability were his sin known. He stands up in the pulpit and delivers sermons calling himself a great sinner, all the while knowing that these words will be interpreted figuratively by his listeners and thus that, far from revealing his sin, they will only further conceal it. Unable to "assign a reason" for his distrust and abhorrence of Chillingworth, he explains away these feelings as products of his general morbid state of mind (140). Although in Dimmesdale the self is more dangerously embroiled in civil war than it is in Hester, the dilemmas of both characters depend on concepts that, though Hawthorne lacks a modern vocabulary to label them, anticipate later psychological understanding.

Notably, too, Hawthorne makes no distinction between men and women in his depiction of mental processes. At this basic level of mind there are no sexual differences. On the other hand, his representation of Hester—not so much of Dimmesdale, except by implication—seems to assume innate psychological differences between men and women. To the extent that *The Scarlet Letter* claims our attention as a work of psychological analysis, this point needs to be pursued. When Hawthorne uses the word *man* for Dimmesdale, it is generally no more than an empty identifier; not so with the term *woman* for Hester. In her case, the word *woman* and its cognates seem to imply a specific female essence.

Sometimes, to be sure, the word is used by characters who have their own individual or cultural ideas of sexual difference. Thus, when Hester first refuses to name her lover, Dimmesdale pays tribute to the "wondrous strength and generosity of a woman's heart" (68); later, as Hester comes into favor with the townspeople through her behavior as a "self-ordained sister of mercy," when they find her helpful, "with power to do, and power to sympathize," they praise her as strong, "with a woman's strength" (161).

But, in chapter 13, "Another View of Hester," the narrator studies her at length in light of what seems presented as an objective, trans-historical ideal of womanhood. On the one hand, she appears to be faulted for having deviated from this ideal (even if she could not help herself); on the other, her good traits appears to be compatible with it. And we cannot fail to note that the worst result of Hester's seven-year isolation, to this narrator, appears to be her loss of beauty—beauty that he describes as attractiveness to men.

"There seemed to be no longer any thing in Hester's face for Love to dwell upon; nothing in Hester's form, though majestic and statue-like, that Passion would ever dream of clasping in its embrace; nothing in Hester's bosom, to make it ever again the pillow of Affection," the narrator says, in a progression increasingly intimate—from desire, to sex, to intimate slumber. And he sums it up: "Some attribute had de-parted from her, the permanence of which had been essential to keep her a woman" (163). This conclusion is reached even while it has been acknowledged that in her errands around town her "nature showed itself warm and rich; a well-spring of human tenderness" (161); and even while her passionate devotion to Pearl is a constant motif in the narration. Thus, it can only be the power to inspire sexual desire in men that Hester has lost; this is what the narrator equates with her essential womanhood. And why is Hester no longer attractive to men? Almost certainly, in view of the narrator's elaboration of her freedom of thought and her independence, it is because she has become alto-gether self-reliant. Thus, we are faced with the irony that a woman is only herself, a woman, if she is an object of the amorous male regard. "Womanhood" and "selfhood" may be incompatible concepts.

Hawthorne develops this paradox at precisely the era in American literary and cultural history when Transcendentalists were firmly preaching self-reliance to all and sundry—but at the same time allo-cating to women the role of dependent helpmate, thus indicating that self-reliance was for men only. In 1844 Margaret Fuller (whom Haw-thorne came to know well while he lived at the Old Manse) wrote an essay on the topic, "The Great Lawsuit," subsequently expanded into a book called *Woman in the Nineteenth Century*, which is generally considered the earliest document in the American woman's rights movement. Fuller argued passionately that until the Transcendentalists expanded their message to include both sexes, their entire program was suspect.

It is evident that Hawthorne has this and other early manifestations of feminism in mind, and that the question of a specifically female psychology was preoccupying him, as it would have to if he were seriously attempting to work with a female protagonist. The first woman's rights convention had been held in 1848, the year before he began to write *The Scarlet Letter;* his sister-in-law Elizabeth Peabody was a feminist; his wife, Sophia, was adamantly antifeminist; one of his sisters (Elizabeth) was feminist in inclination, the other (Maria Louisa) was not. Chapter 13 shows Hester's thoughts moving naturally from her own situation, to Pearl's, to the situation of "the whole race of womankind" (165). The problems—which are real—are not to be overcome "by any exercise of thought," the narrator opines; they cannot be solved; they can only disappear—if and only if the woman's "heart chance to come uppermost" (166).

Hawthorne is not denigrating the quality of Hester's mind here, nor suggesting that women are incapable of thought and ought to leave reasoning to men. Nor is he intending to trivialize her strength, courage, and magnanimity; indeed, the story cannot work without his recognizing these virtues. Yet Hester's character is formed by elements specific to her gender—elements partly enforced on her by society, but partly innate. It is not society's fault that she loves one man and only one passionately and for life, for example; this is part of Hester's womanly nature.

Yet, while Hawthorne makes Hester a real woman in all sorts of ways, he also seems to insist that she isn't one: "Some attribute had departed from her, the permanence of which had been essential to keep her a woman. Such is *frequently* the fate, and such the stern development, of the feminine character and person, when the woman has encountered, and lived through, an experience of peculiar severity" (163, emphasis added). Womanhood, then, is an inalienable essence that is nevertheless completely vulnerable. This contradiction implies that the idea of "woman" is a social construction and, as such, an additional burden on those human beings who must conform to it. The narrator's judgments of Hester vary according to whether she is seen as a person or as a woman, and vary even when she is seen only as a woman: strong with a woman's strength, with the wonderful strength and generosity of a woman's heart, Hester has yet ceased to be a woman! These inconsistencies are perhaps inevitable reflections of the debate over female psychology that the woman's rights movement had precipitated, and that has not yet been concluded.

4

THE SCARLET LETTER
IN *THE SCARLET LETTER*

While some few critics think that Dimmesdale is the main character of *The Scarlet Letter,* most agree that this role belongs to Hester. Yet it could be argued that there is a "character" more important than either of them. According to the dictionary (*Webster's New Collegiate*), the primary meaning of the word *character* is "a conventional graphic device placed on an object as an indication of ownership, age, or relationship," or "a graphic symbol (as a hieroglyph or alphabet letter) used in writing or printing." Taking this primary definition, the chief character in *The Scarlet Letter* must be, of course, the scarlet letter itself. It is typical of Hawthorne's multilayered writing techniques that he should make a symbol that is a character, and a character that is a symbol, and thus utterly confound attempts to derive a single, uncomplicated meaning from his work. In fact, examination of the use of the letter shows that its chief philosophical function is to put in question the very grounds on which one can insist that there is "a" meaning for anything.

As in a hall of mirrors, the letter is reflected, refracted, and duplicated almost endlessly throughout the story. In the scene at Governor Bellingham's house, for example (chapters 7–8), it exists simultaneously in four different versions. Of course, it is there on Hester's dress.

A gross distortion of the letter is reflected in the breastplate of the governor's armor, where it appears "in exaggerated and gigantic proportions, so as to be greatly the most prominent feature of her appearance. In truth, she seemed absolutely hidden behind it" (106). (The symbolism is that to the Puritan rulers, Hester has no identity except in the letter; this means that this distortion of the letter is an accurate reflection of their view of her.) The letter is also represented in Pearl—in fact, twice represented: once in her costume, which Hester has intentionally designed to resemble the letter, "lavishing many hours of morbid ingenuity, to create an analogy between the object of her affection, and the emblem of her guilt and torture" (102); and again in the child herself, for "in truth, Pearl was the one, as well as the other; and only in consequence of that identity had Hester contrived so perfectly to represent the scarlet letter in her appearance" (102).

In the scene of the minister's vigil on the scaffold (chapter 12) the letter is replicated four times, once in each of the characters standing there, and once in the sky. The letter is permanently inscribed in one way or another on Hester, Dimmesdale, and Pearl; it is featured in the sky, repeated in mirrors, eyes, brooks—everywhere one looks, another letter. The word *letter* is inscribed also on the cover of the novel we are reading and, if Hawthorne had gotten his way, would have been doubled on the cover of the novel with a graphic illustration of the *A*. Now the question arises: which one of these multiple appearances is the "real" letter? Are any of these letters counterfeit? Are all of these letters equivalent to each other? Are they basically signs of something "real," something "behind" them, to which they refer and which in turn gives them their meaning?

In his scaffold confession Dimmesdale announces that Hester's external letter, a surface attached to a surface, is only the shadow of the letter branded on his body; and the letter on his body, in turn, is only the "type," the visible indicator, of the letter in his heart. But in order to speak of what is in his heart, Dimmesdale can only speak symbolically. Of course, there isn't really a letter in his heart; there is "something" that he gives a name to but that is certainly not identical to the name, the letter. Nevertheless, even though the letter is not identical to whatever it is made to stand for (whatever is in the heart), the letter is still the only possible way to think and speak about that mysterious and inaccessible interior. In Dimmesdale's view, then, truth resides below the surface, and the surface refers to the hidden truth in some kind of correspondent way. All tangible objects as well as human language are essentially symbolic, referring beyond themselves to some source of meaning. Dimmesdale's "problem," from a philosophical point of view, is that the source is always out of reach; the best one can do is use a symbol, a substitute, for it. A belief that there are sources beyond the symbols can only be expressed through symbols: in the depths of his heart there is only another *A*. If we can never get to the source directly, but only through "mediating" symbols, how can we be sure that the sources really exist? What if there *are* no sources, but only symbols?

The Puritan leaders would not share Dimmesdale's idea that the truth of the letter, the source of its meaning, resides within the human heart. But they certainly share his idea that the letter is no more than a pointer to a truth that is somewhere else. The truth to which the letter refers is in an invisible, divine world: not "inside" the human heart (such a vision, despite Dimmesdale's supposed orthodoxy, is really antinomian), but outside the human being altogether in a place beyond time and change where God has his dwelling. Puritan law, to Puritan rulers, is the representation in "characters" of the divine word. While acknowledging that their law is only a transcription of an original that is somewhere else, they do not doubt the accuracy of their transcription. In devising Hester's particular punishment they plan to mark her in the human world as, in their view, God has already marked her in the invisible world.

Thus, Dimmesdale and the Puritans believe that though truth lies in a world beyond or within the surface where we have to resort to "characters" to represent it, nevertheless a correct representation is possible because there is a fixed and given relation between the representation and the essence for which it stands. Or, differently stated, they do *not* believe that the relation between a truth and its representation is simply arbitrary or conventional, any more than they believe that truth itself is variable.

But both Dimmesdale and the Puritan community are located by Hawthorne in a world that does not mirror their "essentialist" notion of the relation between the sources of meaning and the representation of meaning. To return to the specific question that launched our inquiry, the proliferation of letters in the text of *The Scarlet Letter* makes it very unlikely that there is some "ideal" letter existing outside or inside the surface; insofar as there is one original letter in the novel, the original of which everything else is a better or worse copy, it is not in any specific meaning outside the text but rather in the specific physical object that Hester wears on her gown. That is the letter whose meaning people are concerned about. Constantly, people in the novel are reading it, looking for its symbolic import; yet the letter evades all attempts to fix its meaning and, through such evasion, establishes itself as an entity that is beyond meaning. The letter that Hester wears on her dress is the real letter; all the other visible letters are copies of it; and all interpretations of the letter are not expressions of its truth but—just—interpretations. The question of what that letter "means" is exactly what the story is all about, and the "source" of that story is the physical object, the letter itself, the physical object capable of being read in any number of ways.

But even that physical letter is not a unitary and stable object. By its first appearance it has already deviated from the meaning that the Puritans originally intended it to have. "She hath good skill at her needle . . . but did ever a woman, before this brazen hussy, contrive such a way of showing it! Why, gossips, what is it but to laugh in the faces of our godly magistrates, and make a pride out of what they, worthy gentlemen, meant for a punishment?" (54). When they required her to wear a red *A*, the Puritans assumed that it had one fixed meaning—"adultery." Along with that meaning came a fixed judgment of good or evil. But their view of meaning is shown up as naive at the outset of the story, for at the moment that the tale begins, that supposedly immutable meaning has already been undermined by Hester's artistic and beautiful interpretation of the letter.

Hester's letter, thus, raises two alternative possibilities. First, that the letter has a meaning, but the Puritans, despite their claims to be able to read God's intentions, have got that meaning wrong. Hester herself believes—or comes over time to believe—this alternative. In fact, all the characters in *The Scarlet Letter,* except possibly Pearl, believe it. And if it is true, we are in a pleasant world wherein different meanings of the letter can be proposed and tested, and we can reasonably expect that the "right" meaning will eventually be established.

But the second alternative—that the meaning of the letter is not fixed—is the one that the structure of the novel as a whole seems to validate. And if it is correct, we are in a much more fluid and insecure world, wherein the "meaning" of the letter is not so much a matter of truth as a matter of power: the letter will mean whatever people can be persuaded to believe that it means; it has no fixed and permanent reference.

This is what Hawthorne shows in the novel: a world wherein different individuals and groups are either trying to persuade others that "their" meaning is the right one, or are simply imposing their meaning by physical force (embroidered by plenty of rhetoric and ceremony), while the letter itself remains susceptible to a variety of meanings. He shows this by introducing the letter to us at a point when its meaning is already being questioned, and never from first to last allowing it to be firmly attached to any single meaning. Governor Bellingham's hall of reflecting mirrors aptly epitomizes what happens in this universe of meaning-in-flux: everywhere you look, a different *A,* with a different meaning. The horrid possibility emerges that so many meanings are possible because the *A* itself has no meaning at all, because there is no "*A* itself"; all we have, as modern philosophers would say, is an empty signifier, pure form without content. The mirror symbolism, then, suggests that we live in a world composed entirely of surfaces, and that whatever meaning we find is no more than the meaning we have made.

Not only is the letter in flux at the start, having changed its meaning from the Puritans' original intention at the moment that Hester makes it, but it continues throughout the story as the focus of multiple readings. And as new readings are produced, earlier readings are not discarded; rather, the letter accumulates more and more readings, becomes ever richer in its resonance. And beyond the confines of the novel itself, generations of literary critics and student readers have continued to add meanings beyond those specifically suggested in the story: "able," "admirable," "angel," and so on. In adding meanings, critics are not being untrue to the text; on the contrary, they are following its example in suggesting that the *A* is the locus of indefinite and infinite expansion of meaning.

The letter can easily be read to stand for "art": itself a work of art, its artwork is responsible for subverting the intended Puritan meaning of the letter. It can stand for "artist." It can stand for "author," and "authority," so that Hester is being made to wear the mark of her "adversaries" or "antagonists," while insisting that she will be the "author" of her own letter. Recall the dictionary definition of *character* as "a conventional graphic device placed on an object as an indication of ownership, age, or relationship." In this reading, the letter is a sign that Hester is owned by the Puritan community, and her struggle to change the meaning of the letter is a struggle for her right to "own" herself.

The *A* can stand for Dimmesdale's first name, Arthur, so that we can think of Hester's wearing not only the mark of her illicit act, but the name of her lover, for anybody with eyes to see it. It can stand for "adoration," Hester's emotion for Dimmesdale—an inappropriate emotion, as the story shows, for any human being to feel toward any other. It can stand for "act," a neutral something that, as soon as one names it, becomes value-laden. It can stand for "apple," in reference to the misdeed committed in the Garden of Eden; and, thinking of the Bible account as well as of Puritan theology, we can make it stand for Adam, everyman (and every woman too). It can stand for "alone," or "apart," a condition that the letter certainly creates for its wearer. It can stand for Anne, as in Anne Hutchinson, and for the antinomianism that was her heresy. It can stand for America, as the nation whose origins Hawthorne is examining in *The Scarlet Letter*.

It can remind us of the indefinite article, *a,* as opposed to the definite article *the,* which restricts reference. It can stand for "anything," in another allusion to indefiniteness. As the first letter in the alphabet, it can stand for the alphabet, which means it can stand for "the letter" itself, in another doubling. It can thus symbolize the multiplicity or deceptiveness of "truth" by being simultaneously itself and a symbol of itself, thus containing repetitions and doublings within itself. It can also stand for the law that the Puritans follow and enforce, as in the phrase "the letter of the law"—and in this case it certainly puts the stability of law in question. And in fact, the whole story goes to show that law is constantly in flux.

If the world of *The Scarlet Letter* is one where letters have no fixed meaning, then the conflict between Hester and the Puritans about what her letter means may be seen as a power struggle about whose interpretation is going to prevail—a political struggle not only about the ownership of Hester, but about the far more significant ownership of the letter, which is to say the ownership of language and the law. Certainly, media-conscious people that we have become, we recognize how important it is for any would-be authority to control the manner in which things get said and represented. And this is again to suggest that meaning is arbitrary and determined only as a result of social consensus or by fiat. So long as society is uniform, meanings seem to be fixed, and the relation between a meaning and the character by which it is represented seems to be fixed also. But this is only seeming—as soon as there is heterogeneity, meanings are revealed to be variable and there may be a struggle until consensus is again achieved.

This is the world that we find in *The Scarlet Letter,* with Hester—from a different culture, and of another generation, than the Puritan rulers—standing for the arrival of heterogeneity and the breakdown of consensus. Since the story takes place less than twenty years after the founding of the American colonies, we can see that consensus did not last long; in fact, it may have been a myth in the first place.

Thus, Hawthorne is able to take a single letter of the alphabet and make it stand for multiplicity and the relativity of meaning—to make it stand, in a sense, for anything and everything. He does so even though none of the characters engaged in the struggle to control the letter is a relativist. They sincerely believe that "their" meaning is the correct one, that it rests on stable ground. For the Puritans, stability is in God, and their meanings are thus human representations of divine law. For Hester, stability is in nature, which she takes as the source of a law that competes with Puritan law but is actually prior to it and deserves precedence over it. You could say that nature is Hester's God. To the Puritan plan to take Pearl away from her, she opposes her natural right to the child. In the forest scene when she says to Dimmesdale, "what hast thou to do with these iron men, and their opinions" (197), she is denying that the Puritan law is anything more than opinion; but she does not appeal to a contrasting universe in which anything goes. Instead, she says, "what we did had a consecration of its own" (195), which is to say, what we did was also according to the law, only a different, a higher law from the Puritan law—which, anyway, is only "opinion."

Let us grant that for Hawthorne the Puritans do not have a monopoly on divine law and that what they set out as God's word is in fact the reflection of their own social consensus—in other words, Hawthorne sees Puritan law simply as an expression of the social contract without any divine authorization. Does he agree with Hester that there is a natural law? He has introduced the conflict between social law and natural law in his introductory chapter, "The Prison-Door," through the contrast of the prison, the "black flower of civilized society," with the wild rose bush growing beside its door. That bush is identified both with the antinomian Anne Hutchinson, who denied the relevance of the "moral law," and with "the deep heart of Nature," which can pity and be kind to those whom society has called criminal. Nature looks good.

But over the course of the book it would seem that Hawthorne shows that symbols taken from nature, like the rose bush and the forest, are no more fixed and authoritative in their meanings than the artificial symbols of human letters. The same forest that befriends an innocent child like Pearl is also the abode of the Black Man, whose law is certainly not "higher" than the Puritan law; and it is also the home of the Indian, who has (in Hawthorne's representation) no law at all. Nature, in and of itself, is thoroughly neutral; in order to find law *in* it, one has to impose an interpretation *on* it—which means that you only find in nature the law that you read into it. Such a law is no more authoritative than the law derived from a social consensus. And, as we see from the different outcome for Dimmesdale when he accepts the idea of natural law, it has no authority for anybody but oneself, whereas (at least) a social consensus has validity for numbers of like-minded individuals. Thus, we do not escape from relativism—although we may escape from uncongenial laws—by escaping to nature.

What Hawthorne shows in the plot of *The Scarlet Letter,* then, is not that one or the other idea of the origin of meaning and law is right, whether the origin be in a divine invisible world as the Puritans believed, or in a natural world as Hester (and many nineteenth-century romantics, including such American Transcendentalists as Hawthorne's friends Ralph Waldo Emerson and Henry David Thoreau) believed. The conclusion of *The Scarlet Letter* accords completely with an idea of meaning as a matter of fiat, social negotiation, or consensus. At the end of the story Hester returns to Boston and resumes wearing the letter. Nobody would have required her to wear it any longer, after so much time and so much anguish—which is to say, the law has changed.

But, as a result of her doing so, "the scarlet letter ceased to be a stigma which attracted the world's scorn and bitterness, and became a type of something to be sorrowed over, and looked upon with awe, yet with reverence too" (263). This final meaning for the letter is a compromise, a newly negotiated result. It is not what Hester originally wanted the community to understand by the letter, but it is very far from what the community originally took the letter to mean. The Puritan community has arrived at a new consensus. Hester has not exactly prevailed over them, and she has certainly not been the prophetess of a revolution as she had earlier hopes of being (263). Nevertheless, she has had a powerful effect on her society's system of meanings, which means that she has been an agent of social change. At the end of the story the community is different from what it was at the beginning, and this difference is symbolized by the emergence of a new reading of the letter. People are not quite so judgmental, legalistic, and moralistic as they were at the start. They have recognized a domain of experience that they were earlier unwilling to admit existed. They are beginning to find a language for the heart. They are beginning to recognize the claims of the individual and the claims of women. They are ceasing to be Puritans.

On the other hand, Hester takes up her place at the center of a feminine world where she dispenses consolation and advice with a fairly conservative cast to it. She confines herself to concerns of the lovelorn—no more attacking the foundations of established society. And she counsels patience, promising that there will be a dramatic reconstitution of the relations between men and women "at some brighter period, when the world should have grown ripe for it, in Heaven's own time" (263). This change will be brought about by a woman, but a woman without sin, shame, or even sorrow. It is not difficult to see that such a woman is an impossibility in the world of *The Scarlet Letter* and that, therefore, the world is very far from ripeness. Thus, if the community has moved part of the way toward Hester, she has moved at least as far along the way toward them.

5

THEMES IN
THE SCARLET LETTER

Though there have been stories as long as there have been people, the novel is a relatively recent form. In the nineteenth century, before the advent of film and then television, it was the chief form in which fictions were disseminated to a broad public. For various reasons it was frowned on by serious and educated men. It was dishonest—since the events it recounted had not actually happened; distracting—since it presented worlds more exciting and attractive than the one we live in; damaging—since it unfitted the mind for more serious and tedious kinds of mental activity; addictive—since each novel seemed only to create the desire for more of them. These are only some of the complaints commonly lodged against it.

But as the novel's popularity became ever more firmly established, these same serious men—and women now, too—changed their approach. They began to use the novel for their own, serious purposes. On the thread of an amusing or gripping story they strung thought-provoking issues: philosophical speculations, views of life, moral concerns. And over time it has turned out that, though we read and see and hear thousands of stories in our lifetime, we "study" only those novels that can be read not only for the story, but also for such themes.

This is not to say that, in a serious fiction, story is unimportant. *The*

Scarlet Letter is not a treatise on guilt or on the social construction of meaning. Essentially, first and last, it is a story. But obviously that story is enhanced throughout by its capacity to provoke thought on a range of topics. At every step along the track of the story we are urged to ponder the many ramifications of events and relationships. Hawthorne's symbolic mode requires us to look at events for their larger significance. But rather than thinking that the story exists for the sake of presenting its themes, let us take the opposite approach: the themes exist for the sake of making the story more interesting. Where some novelists add interest to fiction by inventing large numbers of characters, devising many subplots carried out in a diversity of settings and over sweeps of historical time, Hawthorne adds interest by intensifying his basic situation through a technique of enhancing our sense of its significance, its intellectual resonance.

If we wish to divert and refresh ourselves for an hour or more—a natural, healthy, and reasonable desire on all accounts—*The Scarlet Letter* is probably not the book we want. On the other hand, if we hope for a reading experience that will leave us with firm moral messages, absolute truths clearly stated and authoritatively handed down, *The Scarlet Letter* is not the right book, either. For Hawthorne is a storyteller, not a moralist, and had no set doctrine to inculcate; *The Scarlet Letter* is not a piece of didactic fiction. All the mystery, uncertainty, dualities, and ambiguities of his treatment result in calling attention to questions, not enforcing or persuading us to answers. The *A* is ultimately a riddle, teasing and perplexing us. The prevalent mode is inquiring, speculative, meditative. We would make a bad mistake, therefore, if we attempted to simplify *The Scarlet Letter* by translating its themes into messages.

Reduced to its plot elements, the story of *The Scarlet Letter* asks and answers three main questions. Will the separated lovers ever be united? No. Will Dimmesdale's role as Hester's "partner in crime" be revealed? Yes. Will the Puritans ever come to see Hester as she "really" is? Yes and no. From a thematic perspective, however, *The Scarlet Letter* is dense with questions, and it leaves all of them open to a range of answers. Many of these questions have been touched on in earlier parts of this essay: the list to follow recapitulates and adds, but certainly any reader will be able to add to it.

Numerous though they are, all the novel's thematic questions can be seen as rising from the initial situation presented in "The Market-Place," which is that of a supposed division, a rift, in an original unity between individuals and their society. This original unity, however, is immediately exposed as a fantasy because whatever utopia the founders had projected, they quickly had to build a prison. Only fifteen years after the establishment of the "new" society, the prison was already old. The presence of the prison symbolizes the breaking of the law; but if there had really been the imagined unity between individuals and their society, law would have been unnecessary. Law itself, therefore, represents the rift in society, and "individualism" is defined as deviation. The individual, the self, enters the world of *The Scarlet Letter* under a cloud, already judged and marked. In turn, however, the individual attempts to establish her priority to society, and she does this by establishing herself as the center of the law and claiming the right to judge society.

If this is Hester's eventual rationale, it is not Hawthorne's. Far from assuming, as Hester and so many nineteenth-century American romantics did, that the self was prior to society, Hawthorne shows the self as arriving on the scene historically later than society. This is the situation that he represents in "The Market-Place": the moment when an individual emerges from the undifferentiated crowd. To some degree, this is the moment that not only starts the time of *The Scarlet Letter*, but begins American history itself. American history, that is to say, is the record of the idea of the individual. And in a sense it is a moment that begins the idea of history more generally, for there is no history unless people are self-conscious about themselves and wish to keep a record of what happened to them.

And as a fable about the emergence of individualism and history, *The Scarlet Letter* is probably accurate. The consciously elaborated idea of the individual is a relatively modern, Western concept. The newness of the concept does not mean in the least that it is "bad" or "incorrect." Hawthorne, however, given his view of meaning, would probably suppose that the idea has been responsible for creating individuals, rather than individuals being responsible for making the idea. The novel, interestingly enough, has been one of the bulwarks of the idea of the individual. At an abstract level, all novels may be thought of as representing individuals, and hence the concept of individualism, in a great variety of situations. *The Scarlet Letter* raises this representation to a higher level of abstraction, and considers the concept more directly. The concept comes first.

Once the "individual" has emerged as a historical concept, there can be no return to an earlier time. Once we know that we exist, we can never forget it. The moment when we realize that we exist is, for each of us, the beginning of our personal history, and of our sense of historical time. It is also the moment when we become aware of the existence of society, even though we imagine society to be centered on us and to exist chiefly as an aid or an impediment to our demands. A society full of self-aware individuals is, clearly, a different society from one in which the concept does not exist; accordingly, the emergence of individuals requires changes in society. The more powerful the idea of the individual, the greater the pressure will be on society to give an account of itself.

Thereafter, there will always be a clash between the claims of the individual and the claims of society, with each side authorizing its position in numerous ways, including appeals to divine and natural law, and with each compromise only leading to a new separation. *The Scarlet Letter* chronicles one such episode. Each side in the struggle will continuously attempt to extend its territory and power, hoping for nothing less than the ultimate obliteration of the other. Society has, to all appearances, much more power than the individual; but the concept of the individual is so tremendously attractive that it has an unanticipated counterforce of its own. The concept of the individual tells us that our desires are good, that society ought to be organized to enable their satisfaction, and that a proper social organization will allow all our desires to be realized. Once such an idea has taken hold, it cannot be extirpated; despite all its force, the most that society can hope for is to keep it within bounds. Thus, the battle from society's point of view should not be to extirpate individualism, but to contain it, to set boundaries to it. The battle from the individual's point of view, however, may well involve attempting to deny society any right to set boundaries to individuals. Only briefly, in Dimmesdale's return from the forest, does Hawthorne consider what the unbounded individual might look like. He tends, on the whole, to see the battle as unequal, both because society is much more powerful in the force of numbers, and because it has penetrated the individual so deeply that a thoroughly independent self is not really imaginable.

The situation presented in *The Scarlet Letter* raises two questions: where should the boundaries between individual and society be set? and how should the answer to this question be arrived at—that is, what are the proper ways to think about and argue for one position or the other? In the course of the novel Hawthorne suggests many of the arguments that were, in fact, offered on both sides of this debate. Insofar as he has a "position," it is only the general one that neither side can be allowed unlimited power.

From its roots in this duality *The Scarlet Letter* goes on to ask questions about society, the individual, and their possible interrelations.

Society. What is its purpose and justification? Where does it get its power, what kind of power is it, and how is it maintained? If the Puritan belief that society embodies divine command is a delusion, is society the expression of human fantasy? If it does not embody divine law, then whose are the laws that it embodies? If law has no basis in absolutes, how can it be justified? Who "authorizes" "authority"? Are some societies better than others? Is the very concept of society so fragile that no concessions to individuals are allowable?

The individual. Is the individual, in essence, "really" good or "really" bad? Does the idea of the individual as separable from society really make any sense? If people are born into society and only emerge later as individuals, is it not fair to say that "individualism" is a social creation? If so, how can people realistically ever expect to be free of society? We have thought of society as the creation of fantasy, but what if the deepest human feelings are only internalized social prohibitions, like Dimmesdale's profound sense of sin? Is there such a thing as real evil, as distinct from social crime, and if so, how can it be known? If human beings are evil, how can they set themselves up as moral judges? If they are evil, they should be subject to authority external to themselves; but then where does such an authority come from? If they are good, what is the explanation for a society that oppresses them? Are people, perhaps, essential mixtures of good and bad? If so, how can we tell which is which? Where do our ideas of good and bad originate? Is the nature of evil, if evil has a nature, such that a single bad deed colors the entire psyche?

The individual and society. What aspects of individual life should be exempt from social supervision? What is the explanation for feelings of guilt, remorse, conscience? Is sincerity always preferable to hypocrisy? If society is deplorable, why are isolation and alienation so terrible? What is the moral status of love? What is the connection between love and sexual passion? And what about family—is not the secret ideal of *The Scarlet Letter* epitomized in the configuration of father, mother, and child? Would not the best society be one where that configuration was supported by society? And is not that configuration denied by both parties to the struggle between self and society?

Women and society. If, as is obvious, society invests power and authority in males—especially older males—can we not say that society exists to further the individualism of one specific group? And at the expense of other groups? What obligations does society have toward women? and children? How does it justify and maintain the exclusion of women from authority? Are women essentially different kinds of human beings from men? and if so, how is the concept of individualism affected? If women are excluded from society, but also excluded from a concept of individualism, where do they belong? Are we ready to extend the idea of individualism to all human beings regardless of sex? Regardless of whether they are essentially like or unlike one another? Can Hester ever get up on the platform to preach her own sermon rather than to second Dimmesdale's?

The artist. Is the artist necessarily on one side of this struggle or the other? The creative energies that produce art appear to inhere in individuals, not in social groups. Yet, evidently, art can be put to use in the service of society, or in the service of the individual. As an artist, Hester fulfills her own individualistic needs and serves society as well. To some extent she does both at the same time. When the magistrates wear her embroidered collars and cuffs, have they appropriated her gifts, or has she co-opted them?

Historical analysis. As human beings are shaped by their personal pasts, so a nation is shaped by its collective past. And, conversely, individual pasts are developed within a national setting. New England was founded in a particular historical way; its Puritan legacy still exists, Hawthorne believes. It is evidently a legacy of confusion and struggle. The anti-individual Puritans, by virtue of their own break with Old World authority, created the context for an inevitable emergence of individualism. When Dimmesdale sees an *A* in the sky that stands for him, he is only imitating the Puritans' group egotism. They saddle us with our past actions (condemning Hester to wear her letter for life), yet themselves have made (or think they have made) a decisive break with the Old World. They deny that people are free, yet act as though they have freedom. By rooting their view of divine law in their own unauthorized interpretation of the Bible, they invite pluralism. To what extent are we still showing the signs of the struggles they brought with them? Have we kept anything of theirs that we would be better off discarding? If so, are we capable of discarding it? On the other hand, have we thrown overboard anything of theirs that would have been better kept? Isn't their sense that everything matters preferable to our cynicism and nihilism? Is the future of the nation going to be a future of conformity or a future of self-development?

Language, symbolism, and meaning. The Scarlet Letter is profoundly split between the philosophy of its character-actors, who think meaning is stable and externally given (while still struggling to impose *their* meanings on provocative but neutral symbols), and the philosophy of its own structure, which takes meaning to be a matter of arbitrary convention and social negotiation. The struggle for mastery that goes on between Hester and the Puritans focuses with particular urgency on the letter: whose letter is it; who has the right to say what it means? The artist, whom we have noted above as a channel of purely self-expressive and creative energy, has an important role here as a prime manipulator of symbols. Nobody who works with words (Dimmesdale) or images (Hester) is a person whom society can afford to neglect. Even when an artist is not making an overt political statement, the beauty of an artistic production carries a political charge. If it is beautiful, it is supposed to be good. If it is good, it ought to be on "our" side, whichever side we are on. Thus, philosophy quickly becomes politics in *The Scarlet Letter,* and art becomes propaganda.

The human and the natural. Is there anything, finally, that exists outside the human field? If one could imagine Pearl without her *A,* the answer would be yes. But even Pearl, as we see, from the moment of her birth, becomes the object of conflict—from the raw power conflict between Hester and the authorities as to which of them will get to "keep" her, to the more subtle conflict by which both mother and magistrates argue over how to "interpret" her. Pearl, like nature, seems to exist outside the human field; but, like nature, she does so only so long as nobody looks at her. As soon as she is noticed, she falls within the human boundaries and becomes an object of meaning and interpretation.

We are left then to ponder the astonishing finale in which Hester takes Pearl back to Europe and ensures that she marries there. In terms of the themes enunciated, this would appear to be a gesture of turning back the clock and repudiating history. It is, one might say, a thoroughly antinomian gesture, even though Hester then returns to work out her destiny, takes up her letter, and concludes her interrupted struggle with the magistrates. It is also a thoroughly utopian gesture, but how extraordinary to locate utopia in the place that Americans thought they had escaped from. Pearl has been saved—saved from an American future. Does this event imply a statement in favor of individualism or against it? In favor of society or against it? In favor of America or against it? The action of *The Scarlet Letter* comes to a close; but all its questions remain open.

6

THE SCARLET LETTER AND "THE CUSTOM-HOUSE"

When the first draft of *The Scarlet Letter* was about two-thirds complete, Hawthorne set it aside to compose a long introductory sketch. He was concerned that readers would be put off by the unvarying gloom of the novel. He feared that its fantasy and archaisms would not be attractive to readers entranced with realism, at that time a fairly new literary development. His introduction aimed to balance *The Scarlet Letter* with a different kind of writing—more timely, more cheerful, more humorous, more realistic. And the essay developed a context for reading *The Scarlet Letter*. Therefore, it is both a contrast to the novel and an extension of it.

Beyond this, it includes an important discussion of Hawthorne's ideas about writing and about himself as a writer. The passage about the fictional world as a neutral territory has already served us well in considering his setting. Although he focuses his discussion on the text at hand, *The Scarlet Letter*, critics over the years have found "The Custom-House" a key statement about his general literary aims as well as his particular situation as a writer in mid-nineteenth-century America. *The Scarlet Letter* can be read without "The Custom-House," "The Custom-House" without *The Scarlet Letter*. When read together, however, the two produce a whole that is different from either part.

"The Custom-House" contains satirical portraits of real people Hawthorne had worked with in the Salem customhouse. It alludes rather sharply to his political dismissal. Such topical material naturally interested readers of his day, and this along with the humor and satire led many reviewers to prefer it to *The Scarlet Letter*. Remember that before *The Scarlet Letter* Hawthorne published only short sketches under his own name, sketches encompassing a variety of tones and topics. Later critical generations have found his psychological fantasies to be of more worth than his whimsical and satirical pieces, so that the Hawthorne we know well today—what we think of as Hawthorne at his best—is only a selection of the Hawthorne known to his own time. His original readers did not feel that "The Custom-House" detracted from the effect of *The Scarlet Letter* or that its inclusion in the same volume with the longer work was inappropriate. But, since much of what Hawthorne had to say about his writing as well as the particular novel at hand was articulated through his typical allegorical and symbolical methods, the introduction probably did not offer readers much guidance in understanding *The Scarlet Letter*. One had to understand Hawthorne in order to understand his intentions as they were explained in "The Custom-House."

On the surface, "The Custom-House" says that Hawthorne did not invent the story of *The Scarlet Letter*. He found it written up in some old papers on the second floor of the customhouse. He presents himself as the transmitter and editor of someone else's work. In this role, far from retreating from the present back to the past, he is trying to retrieve the past for his readers, helpfully supplementing the archaic text with commentary and explanation.

Of course, this story of discovery is an invention (though not one original to Hawthorne—the device of presenting a novel as an edition of someone's papers is as old as the novel itself). Trained readers would not have been fooled for an instant, and to make sure that even the most inexperienced among them knew what he was about, Hawthorne wrote, "I must not be understood as affirming that, in the dressing up of the tale, and imagining the motives and modes of passion that influenced the characters who figure in it, I have invariably confined myself within the limits of the old Surveyor's half a dozen sheets of foolscap. On the contrary, I have allowed myself, as to such points, nearly or altogether as much license as if the facts had been entirely of my own invention" (33). Hawthorne undermines the veracity of his account of discovering the papers on the second floor of the customhouse. Why? Only to lead us to ask: since we are not supposed to believe it, what is the purpose of this invention?

Let us, therefore, look more closely at the extensive preparation that Hawthorne provides, in "The Custom-House," for this discovery of the scarlet letter, symbolically the discovery of his literary subject. This preparation constitutes nothing more than an imaginative autobiographical account of why Hawthorne went to work in the customhouse in the first place, and what befell him there. Briefly, he says that he returned to Salem and worked in the customhouse to satisfy the ghosts of his Puritan ancestors, who disapproved of his literary vocation. "'What is he?' murmurs one gray shadow of my forefathers to the other. 'A writer of story-books! What kind of a business in life,—what mode of glorifying God, or being serviceable to mankind in his day and generation,—may that be? Why, the degenerate fellow might as well have been a fiddler!'" (10).

Despite his sincere intentions to put aside writing and engage in the life of his own day and age, Hawthorne found the work boring and the routine deadening. His manhood seemed to be seeping away. The other employees of the customhouse (who are described in extended and satirical detail) were as good as dead already. One day, when business was light, he was browsing through old papers in the upper story and found a manuscript wrapped around a "rag of scarlet cloth" which, on inspection, proved to be the letter *A* finely embroidered with gold thread (31). The letter intrigued him. "Certainly, there was some deep meaning in it, most worthy of interpretation, and which, as it were, streamed forth from the mystic symbol, subtly communicating itself to my sensibilities, but evading the analysis of my mind" (31). Having read through *The Scarlet Letter,* we shall be pleased but not surprised to find the motif of meaning and interpretation introduced simultaneously with the letter.

The papers in which the letter was wrapped turn out to contain the outlines of the story of a woman's life, the woman cagily described as one "who appeared to be rather a noteworthy personage in the view of our ancestors" (32). Hawthorne accepted—what he interpreted as a summons from the long-dead writer of these papers—the obligation to work up her story for publication. Unfortunately, the oppression of life in the customhouse was so great that he could not carry out his promise. "An entire class of susceptibilities, and a gift connected with them,—of no great richness or value, but the best I had,—was gone from me" (36).

Not until he was dismissed from the customhouse did he find himself able to write the story. Thus, traumatic though it was to lose his job ("the moment when a man's head drops off is seldom or never, I am inclined to think, precisely the most agreeable of his life" [41]), it had the result of restoring him to his true vocation. While the press carried on over his "decapitation," Hawthorne, "with his head safely on his shoulders," had made "an investment in ink, paper, and steel-pens, had opened his long-disused writing-desk, and was again a literary man" (43). Hawthorne's story ends with his departure from Salem and his successful completion of the story of the scarlet letter.

Among several points worthy of notice in considering this imaginary autobiographical narrative, perhaps the most important in connection with *The Scarlet Letter* is its structural duplication of Hester's situation. Like Hester, Hawthorne is in conflict with Puritans. They disapprove of what he does and mark him (internally) with their disapproval. He attempts to conform his life to their rules and to adopt their judgments. But his attempt fails; try as he may, he cannot share their estimate of his literary ambitions, and he is increasingly aware that what they would define out of his existence is nothing less than the very principle of that existence. To accept their judgments, to live by their law, is to die.

The upper story of the customhouse can be seen as analogous to the forest, where there is an escape from human law. Hawthorne's fascination with the letter can be understood as his intuitive understanding that it is "his" letter; and, indeed, while wondering about its import, he (accidentally, of course) puts it on his breast. "It seemed to me, then, that I experienced a sensation not altogether physical, yet almost so, as of burning heat; and as if the letter were not of red cloth, but red-hot iron" (32). At this moment, Hester and Hawthorne (whose shared initial may not be merely coincidence) are identified as the same person. Come to think of it, isn't Hester, like Hawthorne, an artist? And isn't Hawthorne's book, which he had hoped to publish with a red *A* on the cover, his defiant answer to the Puritans? A double answer—in that it represents his return to a despised profession and, moreover, the commitment of his art to the defense of an outcast woman. In pursuit of this analogy we can even go so far as to suggest that leaving Salem and publishing *The Scarlet Letter* are equivalent to Hester's leaving Boston and bringing Pearl to adulthood as "a citizen of somewhere else" (44).

If "The Custom-House" identifies Hester with her creator, we have to suppose that *The Scarlet Letter* carries an intense autobiographical charge. As a story, it embroiders and beautifies, and at length—and irresistibly—it justifies Hester's *A*. As a work of literature, it is Hawthorne's defense of himself and his art. And this art proceeds from a deliberate, long-gestated decision to reject the right of those in authority to determine the course of his life by imposing their moral judgments on him. What he did had a consecration of its own.

In defending his right to live against the right of authorities to tell him how to live, Hawthorne works within the same personal and emotive domain as Hester does at first. But just as her personal situation leads her to ever more general and abstract ideas, so Hawthorne's personal situation as the artist in the customhouse is susceptible to generalization. "Hawthorne in the customhouse" is interpretable, symbolically, as a representation of the situation of the artist in America. For by the middle of the nineteenth century the nation was vigorously representing itself, in the press and in public oratory, as devoted to business, free enterprise, the practical, the useful. And as a democracy, it was very much attuned to consensus and conformity. The savagery of Puritan intolerance was a thing of the past, but the individual who stood out in a crowd was still seen not merely as different, but very likely as blameworthy for being so. The person who, in an energetic commercial society, prefers to create works of art, who dreams instead of calculating, feels stigmatized for that preference. (Perhaps we see here some explanation of Pearl's return to Europe, as well as her marriage to an aristocrat—another *A* word.) In the Old World, marks of difference can be marks of distinction. The artist has no place in the customhouse: that is Hawthorne's symbolic statement.

In defending himself, then, Hawthorne suggests that the democratic and commercial American nation has found no place for the artist, has indeed excluded the artist from its roll call of legitimate citizens. We can go further still in such an interpretation and take the artist himself or herself as personifying the human qualities that art requires for its creation: creativity, originality, imagination, the love of beauty. Then "The Custom-House" proposes that the nation has no place or respect for such qualities. The essay becomes a passionate defense of the imagination and creativity in a country that has no use for them.

Because Hawthorne is standing up for "pure" imagination, he rejects the compromise that is available to artists in America, which is to write "realistic" works. Work of this sort makes imagination serve the real world, enforcing its claims upon us, making us forget how much our own fantasies have entered into the construction of what we accept as objective reality. Hawthorne provides some samples of realistic writing in "The Custom-House" in his description of his colleagues. Therefore, we know that when he writes a piece like *The Scarlet Letter* it is not because he is incapable of literary realism; it is a matter of choice. A true defense of imagination calls for a total commitment. (Under the circumstances, how ironic it is that these same descriptions were thought, by some, to be superior to *The Scarlet Letter*. Ironic, or perhaps only what Hawthorne would have expected.)

To some degree, the stance that he takes in "The Custom-House" is more utopian than that adopted by Hester at the end of *The Scarlet Letter*. She brought the community around partly by investing herself in altruistic deeds of social service, whereas Hawthorne takes a stand on nothing short of absolute dedication to his art. On the one hand, he seems to want to imply that any notion that there is "only" a real world is self-delusion; on the other, that such a world could quite possibly come into existence, but it would be totalitarian. These two apparently incompatible statements can be reconciled at another level of discourse by understanding that a totalitarian society has simply granted all authority to its own particular fantasies and outlawed everybody else's. Outlawed fantasies acquire tremendous destructive force—witness the devil in the forest. A society more open to imaginative variety is at once a richer, more satisfying place to live, and a safer—ironically, a more substantial—one. The survival of a real world depends upon the survival of imaginative freedom within it. Artists serve the world, and the democratic cause, after all, by declaring their independence from majority rule.

Bibliography of Selected Primary Works

EDITIONS OF HAWTHORNE'S WORKS

The Centenary Edition of the Works of Nathaniel Hawthorne. William Charvat, Roy Harvey Pearce, and Claude M. Simpson, general editors. Columbus: Ohio State University Press, 1964–. Sixteen volumes have appeared to date, including all the tales, romances, sketches, and children's writings, drafts of the late unfinished stories, as well as the American, French, and Italian Notebooks and early letters. Still to be published are the English Notebooks, the later letters, and miscellaneous writings.

BOOKS

Fanshawe: A Tale. Boston: Marsh & Capen, 1828.

Twice-Told Tales. Boston: American Stationers Co., 1837.

Grandfather's Chair. Boston: E. P. Peabody; New York: Wiley & Putnam, 1841.

Biographical Stories for Children. Boston: Tappan & Dennet, 1842.

Twice-Told Tales (expanded edition). Boston: James Munroe & Co., 1842.

Mosses from an Old Manse. New York, Wiley & Putnam, 1846.

The Scarlet Letter: A Romance. Boston: Ticknor, Reed, & Fields, 1850.

The House of the Seven Gables. Boston: Ticknor, Reed, & Fields, 1851.

True Stories from History and Biography. Boston: Ticknor, Reed, & Fields, 1851.

The Snow-Image, and Other Twice-Told Tales. Boston: Ticknor, Reed, & Fields, 1852.

A Wonder-Book for Girls and Boys. Boston: Ticknor, Reed, & Fields, 1852.

The Blithedale Romance. Boston: Ticknor, Reed, & Fields, 1852.

Life of Franklin Pierce. Boston: Ticknor, Reed, & Fields, 1852.

Tanglewood Tales for Girls and Boys. Boston: Ticknor, Reed, & Fields, 1853.

Mosses from an Old Manse. Revised edition. Boston: Ticknor & Fields, 1854.

The Marble Faun, or, The Romance of Monte Beni. Boston: Ticknor & Fields, 1860.

Our Old Home. Boston: Ticknor & Fields, 1863.

Bibliography of Selected Secondary Works

BIOGRAPHY

Loggins, Vernon. *The Hawthornes: The Story of Seven Generations of an American Family.* New York: Columbia University Press, 1951.

Mellow, James R. *Nathaniel Hawthorne in His Times.* Boston: Houghton Mifflin Company, 1979.

Stewart, Randall. *Nathaniel Hawthorne: A Biography.* New Haven: Yale University Press, 1948.

Turner, Arlin. *Nathaniel Hawthorne: A Biography.* New York: Oxford University Press, 1979.

CRITICAL STUDIES: BOOKS

Arvin, Newton. *Hawthorne.* Boston: Little, Brown, 1929.
Biographical study focusing on Hawthorne's alienation.

Baym, Nina. *The Shape of Hawthorne's Career.* Ithaca: Cornell University Press, 1976.
All of Hawthorne's works considered in chronological order, tracing his professional development.

Bell, Michael Davitt. *Hawthorne and the Historical Romance of New England.* Princeton: Princeton University Press, 1971.
Discusses historical novels about New England written in Hawthorne's day, and compares them to Hawthorne's works.

Bell, Millicent. *Hawthorne's View of the Artist.* Albany: State University of New York Press, 1962.
Study of artists and artist figures in all of Hawthorne's works.

Byers, John R., Jr., and Owen, James J. *A Concordance to the Five Novels of Nathaniel Hawthorne.* 2 vols. New York: Garland Publishing, 1979.
Alphabetical listing of all occurrences of every word in Hawthorne's novels; extremely useful research tool.

Chase, Richard. *The American Novel and Its Tradition.* New York: Anchor Books, 1957.
Establishes Hawthorne's type of fiction as a "romance," essentially different from the English realistic "novel."

Cohen, B. Bernard, ed. *The Recognition of Nathaniel Hawthorne: Selected Criticism since 1828.* Ann Arbor: University of Michigan Press, 1969.
A collection of important criticism through the years.

Colacurcio, Michael J., ed. *New Essays on The Scarlet Letter.* Cambridge: Cambridge University Press, 1985.
Hawthorne as profound student of the Puritan era.

Crews, Frederick C. *The Sins of the Fathers: Hawthorne's Psychological Themes.* New York: Oxford University Press, 1966.
A Freudian interpretation of Hawthorne's works.

Crowley, J. Donald, ed. *Hawthorne: The Critical Heritage.* New York: Barnes and Noble, 1970.
A collection of important critical essays and early reviews.

Erlich, Gloria. *The Tenacious Web: Family Themes in Hawthorne's Fiction.* New Brunswick, N.J.: Rutgers University Press, 1984.
Study of themes of the family in Hawthorne's works as shaped by his growing up in the Manning household.

Feidelson, Charles. *Symbolism and American Literature.* Chicago: University of Chicago Press, 1953.
Hawthorne as a symbolist and pioneer of modernist literary techniques, especially in his use of the scarlet letter.

Fogle, Richard Harter. *Hawthorne's Fiction: The Light and the Dark.* Norman: University of Oklahoma Press, 1964.
Patterning of Hawthorne's imagery and symbolism discussed to bring out his techniques and his worldview.

Male, Roy R. *Hawthorne's Tragic Vision.* Austin: University of Texas Press, 1957.
Hawthorne as a humanist with a tragic vision of humanity.

Martin, Terence. *Nathaniel Hawthorne.* Revised edition. Boston: Twayne Publishers, 1983.
An extremely useful and well-written general introduction to Hawthorne's life and writings.

Schubert, Leland. *Hawthorne the Artist*. Chapel Hill: University of North Carolina Press, 1944.
Study of Hawthorne's techniques.

Waggoner, Hyatt H. *Hawthorne: A Critical Study*. Cambridge, Mass.: Harvard University Press, 1955.
Hawthorne as a Christian opposed to the optimism of his time.

CRITICAL STUDIES: ARTICLES

Baym, Nina. "Thwarted Nature: Nathaniel Hawthorne as Feminist." In *American Novelists Revisited: Essays in Feminist Criticism,* edited by Fritz Fleischmann, 58–77. Boston: G. K. Hall, 1982.
A feminist approach to Hawthorne's women characters and their situations vis-á-vis men and authority.

Colacurcio, Michael J. "Footsteps of Anne Hutchinson: The Context of *The Scarlet Letter.*" *ELH: A Journal of English Literary History* 39(1973):459–94.
Well-informed consideration of the relation between Anne Hutchinson's doctrinal quarrel with the Puritans, and its implications for Hawthorne's attitude toward Hester.

Eisinger, Chester E. "Hawthorne as Champion of the Middle Way." *New England Quarterly* 27(1954):27–52.
Hawthorne's ideal is one of balance.

Martin, Terence. "Dimmesdale's Ultimate Sermon." *Arizona Quarterly* 27(1971):230–40.
Dimmesdale's psychology as man and Puritan, especially as revealed in the last scaffold scene.

Newberry, Frederick. "Tradition and Disinheritance in *The Scarlet Letter.*" *ESQ: A Journal of the American Renaissance* 23(1977):1–26.
Pertinent English history at the time of the action of *The Scarlet Letter.*

Reynolds, Larry J. "*The Scarlet Letter* and Revolution Abroad." *American Literature* 57(1985):44–67.
Discussion of contemporary historical events reflected in *The Scarlet Letter,* especially the French Revolution of 1848.

Ryskamp, Charles. "The New England Sources of *The Scarlet Letter.*" *American Literature* 31(1959):257–72.
The most authoritative study of Hawthorne's sources for, and use of, New England history in *The Scarlet Letter.*

Index

Index

About the Author

Nina Baym is director of the School of Humanities and professor of English at the University of Illinois, Urbana-Champaign. She is the author of three books on nineteenth-century American fiction: *The Shape of Hawthorne's Career* (1976); *Woman's Fiction: A Guide to Novels by and about Women in America, 1820–1870* (1978); and *Novels, Readers, and Reviewers: Responses to Fiction in Antebellum America* (1984). In addition she has written numerous scholarly essays and reviews on American authors and American literary topics. Holder of fellowships from the Guggenheim Foundation and the National Endowment for the Humanities, she has served on the editorial boards of several journals including *American Quarterly, American Literature, New England Quarterly, Legacy,* and *Tulsa Studies in Women's Literature.*